SHACKLETON'S
ENDURANCE

Also by Joanna Grochowicz

Into the White
Amundsen's Way

SHACKLETON'S ENDURANCE

AN ANTARCTIC SURVIVAL STORY

JOANNA GROCHOWICZ

ALLEN&UNWIN
SYDNEY・MELBOURNE・AUCKLAND・LONDON

First published by Allen & Unwin in 2021

Allen & Unwin
83 Alexander Street
Crows Nest NSW 2065
Australia
Phone: (61 2) 8425 0100
Email: info@allenandunwin.com
Web: www.allenandunwin.com

A catalogue record for this book is available from the National Library of Australia

ISBN 978 1 76052 609 2

For teaching resources, explore www.allenandunwin.com/resources/for-teachers

Cover and text design by Joanna Hunt
Cover and text illustrations by Sarah Lippett
Set in 11/17.5 pt ITC Legacy Serif by Midland Typesetters, Australia
Printed in Australia in February 2022 by McPherson's Printing Group

10 9 8 7 6 5 4 3

www.joannagrochowicz.com

The paper in this book is FSC® certified. FSC® promotes environmentally responsible, socially beneficial and economically viable management of the world's forests.

For Pawel

IMPERIAL TRANS-ANTARCTIC EXPEDITION

Trans-continental party

Sir Ernest Shackleton – Leader**

Frank Wild – Deputy***

Frank Hurley – Photographer*

Dr Alexander 'Mack' Macklin – Surgeon

George 'Putty' Marston – Artist*

Tom Crean – Second Officer**

The *Endurance*

Frank 'The Skipper' Worsley – Captain of the *Endurance*

Lionel Greenstreet – First Officer

Hubert Hudson – Navigator

Henry 'Chippy' McNish – Carpenter

Thomas Orde-Lees – Motor expert

Dr James 'Mick' McIlroy – Doctor

Lewis Rickinson – Chief Engineer

Alexander Kerr – Assistant Engineer

Charles Green – Cook

Perce Blackborow – Stowaway

Seamen:

William Bakewell

Alf Cheetham***

Ernie Holness

Walter How

Timothy McCarthy

Thomas McLeod*

John Vincent

William Stephenson

Scientists

James Wordie – Geologist and chief scientist

Robert Clark – Biologist

Leonard Hussey – Meteorologist

Reginald 'Jimmy' James – Physicist

* number of previous expeditions to Antarctica

KEY DATES

1914

8 August – *Endurance* leaves Britain

26 October – *Endurance* leaves Buenos Aires

5 November – *Endurance* arrives in South Georgia

5 December – *Endurance* leaves South Georgia

30 December – *Endurance* crosses the Antarctic Circle

1915

19 January – *Endurance* is caught in ice

27 October – Shackleton gives the order to abandon ship

21 November – *Endurance* sinks

23 December – the men leave Ocean Camp

29 December – the men establish Patience Camp

1916

23 March – land is sighted from Patience Camp

9 April – the men take to the boats

15 April – the men reach Elephant Island (Cape Valentine)

17 April – the men relocate to Cape Wild

24 April – *James Caird* leaves Elephant Island

10 May – *James Caird* arrives in South Georgia

19 May – Shackleton, Worsley and Crean set off from King Haakon Sound

20 May – Shackleton, Worsley and Crean arrive in Stromness

23 May – *Southern Sky* leaves South Georgia

10 June – *Instituto de Pesca No 1* leaves the Falkland Islands

12 July – *Emma* leaves Punta Arenas

25 August – *Yelcho* leaves Punta Arenas

30 August – Shackleton, Worsley and Crean arrive in Elephant Island aboard *Yelcho*

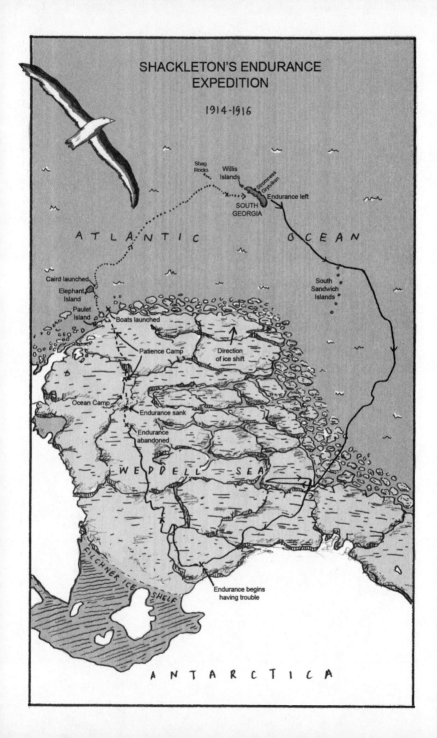

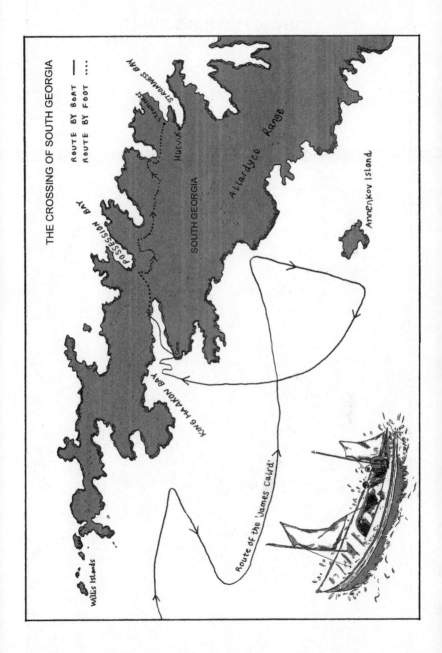

THE CROSSING OF SOUTH GEORGIA

ROUTE BY BOAT ——
ROUTE BY FOOT ····

POSSESSION BAY

STROMNESS BAY
Stromness
Husvik
SOUTH GEORGIA
Allardyce Range

KING HAAKON BAY

Willis Islands

Annenkov Island

Route of the 'James Caird'

'THE LAST GREAT POLAR JOURNEY'

The explorer has known moments of great excitement and this is one of them. Failing to convey the sheer scale of his ambition in words, he takes up a pen and draws a map of the continent on the back of a menu. Nothing more than an empty circle. With a line drawn through it. This is the plan he shares at the geological society lunch.

'I believe it will take one hundred and twenty days,' he says. 'One short Antarctic summer.'

His assertion is met with raised eyebrows. The gentlemen at the lunch who might be persuaded to fund such a venture are intrigued but not yet convinced.

The game has changed. The pole has been conquered. Captain Scott is dead and Roald Amundsen is victorious. For so long Sir Ernest Shackleton imagined himself at 90 degrees south. But getting to the only place on earth where all directions point north is not enough now. Another more ambitious venture awaits: to cross the Antarctic continent from the Weddell Sea to the Ross Sea. At almost 3000 kilometres, it will be the 'last great polar journey to be made'. Much of the terrain they will cover is uncharted, probably pockmarked with obstacles. In his optimistic way, Shackleton hopes to finally leave his mark on the continent.

The fight will be a good one. Third time lucky. He knows from experience that planning takes years; finding money takes courage. Exploration costs a great deal and the 39-year-old explorer has no riches of his own. He has charm though, bags of it. Having dealt out a large amount of it over lunch, he leaves the function more determined than ever.

Next Shackleton applies his talents to securing the backing of prominent institutions, ingratiating himself with sponsors, gladhanding politicians, royalty and society ladies. Months of back slapping, asking favours, and making promises that he hopes to keep has left him exhausted and in poor health. But his efforts pay off with a fine ship, men, sledge dogs and enough provisions to last several years.

The Imperial Trans-Antarctic Expedition sets sail from Britain on 8 August 1914, even as Germany enters into conflict with Russia, then France, and general mobilisation is ordered in England. He feels obliged to offer his ship to the Royal Navy and release his men, but the Admiralty tells him to set sail for British glory. Nothing, not even the outbreak of world war, will hold Shackleton back.

The expedition is still short of funds and money must be borrowed. Shackleton wants his men's wages to go to their families during their long absence. Ultimately, any debts can be repaid by selling the story to the newspapers on his return. Everybody loves reading about daring individuals cheating death while they sip tea over breakfast. As it turns out there's money in suffering. Shackleton only hopes that on the 'last great polar journey' there will not be too much of it.

Part I

Idealism

CHAPTER ONE

ARGENTINA, OCTOBER 1914

The Buenos Aires docks are a busy place. There's the usual activity of boats arriving and departing, fishing vessels offloading their catch, cargo ships undergoing repairs, others taking on supplies and crew. There's shouting in every language, bustle and muck, donkeys hitched to wooden carts and a stray dog looking for handouts but receiving a kick.

Aside from the odd malingerer, most of the men hanging around are looking for work. Their faces are haggard from toil and weather and fighting. Some are local, others are from as far away as the British Isles – hardy seafarers, looking to work their passage home so they can sign up. A dose of ground warfare in Europe would make a nice change from doing battle in the Southern Seas.

Others can think of nothing worse than being stuck on dry land. They have sea fever. For them, life only has meaning if it can be spent in wind, on waves, sailing the deep. They long for fresh air and dream of adventure. One ship in particular captures their imagination. It's a British vessel, on its way to Antarctica. The dockside dreamers peer up at the *Endurance*, hoping for a glimpse of the polar hero. With his large square face, hair parted down the middle of his head, he's unmistakeable. Sir Ernest Shackleton is often on deck arranging things, directing men, laughing like he hasn't a care in the world.

Down on the wharf, the chatter is a mix of fact and hearsay. 'What's he planning now?'

'To walk across Antarctica.'

'Been done.'

'No it hasn't. You're thinking of the south pole. That's only halfway across.'

'The Norwegian. He did it.'

'Yeah, and Scott died trying.'

'You wouldn't get me trying.'

'Or dying, trying.'

One young enthusiast, Perce Blackborow, has stopped Shackleton twice in the street to ask for work. Supposedly eighteen years old, he doesn't look a day over fifteen. Perhaps that's why Shackleton always has a ready smile for him.

'I'm a hard worker and a quick learner,' Blackborow declares with force.

'Of course you are,' Shackleton replies warmly. 'But you're also too young.'

Two refusals and still Blackborow stands there, admiring the black hull of the *Endurance*, engaging whoever comes sauntering down the gangplank, hoping for an opportunity to prove his worth to 'the Boss', as everyone calls Shackleton. Mostly the boy is a figure of pity.

'Just look at the tragic expression on his face,' says one of the crew. 'Perhaps we should take the lad with us.'

'That'd be throwing him in the deep end,' says Frank Wild. 'He needs some hair on his chest before he heads south.'

Wild rolls up his shirtsleeves to reveal brown arms and merchant navy tattoos – a snake on one arm and an anchor on the other. Up until now Shackleton's second-in-command has had to content himself with managing expedition business from behind a desk. He'd far rather be here in the fresh air, manhandling crates and seeing to sledge dogs. But there are a few issues to sort out before they set sail for South Georgia and then Antarctica. The Boss, newly arrived from London, is not happy.

The Imperial Trans-Antarctic Expedition is a shambles. The ship has a leak, there's no coal for the boilers nor a cook for the galley, vital supplies are missing, and they're four sailors short. Worst of all, nobody seems concerned, not even the captain.

Unlike Frank Wild, Captain Frank 'The Skipper' Worsley has never been south. He certainly wasn't Shackleton's first choice, although he does have decades of experience on the sea. Frank Wild remembers the first time he met the unconventional New Zealander at the expedition offices in London. Worsley bounded in the door grinning, and proudly announced that he'd navigated a ship through ice on New Burlington Street in a dream and had come looking for a job there as soon as he woke up. Wild wasn't persuaded by the story but Worsley did show up at the right time to convince the Boss of his worthiness.

The captain's not the only questionable hire. There have been plenty of other arbitrary choices among those selected to take part in the expedition. Sometimes Wild looks around the deck at the hardened seafarers, the toffs, the merchant navy men, and the wet ones who have never ventured beyond a university campus, and wonders if a more mismatched group of individuals has ever been assembled.

When Worsley returns to the *Endurance* from his errand down on the docks, he raises both arms in triumph. After making a few enquiries on shore he's found Charles Green, a man he thinks can replace their old cook – the one who has just been fired for drunken behaviour. The captain hopes the Boss approves of his choice. Options are few. To be sure, there are others who could do the job but very few of the men Worsley has spoken to are interested in going so far south. And on a voyage of such a duration.

'Can you cook?' Shackleton asks.

'They seemed to think so.' Green cocks his head in the direction of the cargo vessel at the end of the pier, a filthy rust-bucket of a thing.

'How do you feel about the cold?'

Green shrugs. 'Exactly the same way I feel about the wet.'

Shackleton is yet to meet a sailor who complains about getting a soaking. 'Fix a few meals and if you don't poison us with your cooking, you've got yourself a job.'

In typical Shackleton fashion, the interview is a short one.

Watching as yet another man is taken aboard the *Endurance*, Perce Blackborow thrusts his hands in his pockets. He's taken up smoking, a habit he hoped would make him look manly, but it has done little beyond getting him on first-name terms with the crew. Most of these men are happy to help smoke the boy's tobacco, but care little for his desire to join them on their polar escapade. The ship's cat shows more genuine friendship.

Recognising Blackborow as a permanent fixture at the end of the gangplank, the cat twists its tortoiseshell body between his legs. The young man likes the cat but he doesn't like the cat's owner. The ship's carpenter is an old curmudgeon with a broad Scottish accent. Everyone calls him Chippy, but he's really Henry McNish. The cat is utterly devoted to Chippy. Blackborow supposes that this is why the cat is called Mrs Chippy, although she is obviously a he. Blackborow may be inexperienced, but there's nothing wrong with his powers of observation.

It is a spring day in late October when the *Endurance* finally pulls away from the dock. Shackleton is impatient to be off, to leave behind the crowds of well-wishers, the Argentine officials, the brass band and its rambunctious medley, and his unresolved money worries. There are few perils in the southern wilds that he cannot face with confidence and yet so many sources of stress on dry land. Having felt so poorly in recent weeks, Shackleton longs for the fresh air of the open water to set him right. It always does. There are two doctors on board, but he has no intention of allowing either Dr Macklin or Dr McIlroy to examine him. Nothing good will come of it. This is a time for boldness, not cures.

South Georgia is their next and final stop. From there the *Endurance* will head south to the Weddell Sea, where men and stores will be dropped at Vahsel Bay on the Antarctic coast to commence their 3000-kilometre journey across the continent immediately.

For now, they have all they need: strong winds, a cloudless sky, and coal in reserve. After more than two weeks in Buenos Aires refitting the ship, everyone feels the excitement of the southern journey building. Even the sixty-nine sledge dogs, chained up to shipboard kennels, close their eyes against the sun and thrust their snouts windward in a way that can only express the deepest contentment.

Photographer Frank Hurley contemplates the horizon and wonders what adventures lie before him on this, his second voyage to Antarctica. His camera is already at work. *There's the book to consider*, he thinks with satisfaction, remembering how Shackleton pitched the idea of documenting their journey. What a thrill, to have been invited along by the polar hero. When he thinks of all he had to do to convince Douglas Mawson to take him on his Antarctic expedition in 1911. Offering to work without pay! How like that desperate lad standing by the gangplank in Buenos Aires.

The dogs are appealing subjects for the photographer and the *Endurance* is a beautiful ship when in full sail. The three-masted wooden vessel is sturdy but utterly reliant on her coal-powered steam engines. Originally built as tourist ship in Norway, she is not ideally suited to long voyages. The Boss says she's sluggish. He prefers his last ship, the *Nimrod*, and wonders if this one has what it takes to get through the pack ice. Now Shackleton is on board, the crew are hard at work and smile whenever they see Hurley's camera. The scientists too are doing their part, learning the ropes and doing a passable job when not throwing up over the side. Everyone needs to pitch in when the ship is undermanned, all twenty-seven men, including the Boss.

There's another pair of hands, well hidden, but only discovered three days into the journey. When Blackborow is pulled from the fo'c'sle and the cries of '*Stowaway!*' ring out, most of the sailors are very pleased at the thought of extra help. The boy is seasick and horribly dehydrated but eager to prove his worth. Mostly he is pleased to finally be allowed out from the locker where a couple of well-intentioned sailors concealed him. On seeing the wide open sea, Blackborow beams with delight. Despite enduring a great deal of discomfort, the boy has not cracked or given himself up. He certainly hasn't revealed his accomplices. Such pluck is to be admired.

The Boss shouts: 'If we run out of food and someone has to be eaten, it will be you first! Do you understand?'

But it's all a grand show rather than genuine displeasure. In fact, the Boss must turn quickly away to hide a smile. He recognises himself in the lad. Given half a chance at that age, he'd have done exactly the same thing.

CHAPTER TWO

SOUTH GEORGIA, NOVEMBER 1914

The odour hits them first. Evil and intense, the smell of slaughter arrives on the evening breeze while the oily spoils cling to the waves like a disease. The dogs come out of their kennels, suddenly alert, their nostrils twitching with excitement. The men spit over the side, desperate to rid their mouths of the unpleasant taste. Are the factories with their plumes of smoke the source of the stench, or is it the rotting mounds of offal on the shoreline that smell so putrid?

The pilot vessel guiding the *Endurance* into the bay chugs happily past the floating whale carcasses awaiting flensing. The bodies look like enormous dark sausages fit to burst. The seamen talk in low voices. There's general agreement: this must be the smelliest place on earth. The scientists gape, appalled but also fascinated by a whaling station in full swing. Welcome to Grytviken, South Georgia.

The whalers of Grytviken are a hardy breed, mostly of Scandinavian origin. They live a bleak existence at the end of the earth. Not many visitors pass by this way, but those who do get a very warm reception. When the *Endurance* drops anchor, the crew are welcomed ashore as brothers. There is much to discuss with these brave souls who ply their dangerous trade where other men fear to venture.

The whalers' knowledge of the southern seas is unrivalled. It is therefore with extreme disappointment that Shackleton learns that, even though it is late spring, navigation through to the Weddell Sea is currently impossible due to the slow break-up of the winter sea ice. It's the worst possible news. The *Endurance* will have to wait in South Georgia for more favourable conditions. The original plan had them starting the Antarctic crossing by the beginning of December, but realistically it will be December before they can consider leaving South Georgia.

This means they will not have nearly enough time to complete the journey. Nobody wants to find themselves in the middle of the continent when winter sets in. And as for the ship, which was supposed to return to South Georgia after dropping them off; there are questions around that part of the plan too.

'It might be best if the ship stays with us over winter, Frank,' says Shackleton to Wild. 'At least we can use the time to get everything ready to start out early next Antarctic spring.'

Wild looks dubious. It's a risky proposition for a ship to be frozen in, as they both know. Regardless, Shackleton can see clear benefits.

'If the ship overwinters in the ice, the scientists will have a place to carry out some of their work. In case we fail, we must have something to show for our troubles.'

Wild scratches his beard thoughtfully. After a pause, he says, 'Remember how tightly *Discovery* was held?'

He hardly needs to remind the Boss of his first expedition to Antarctica; it's when the two men first met. The ship was very nearly abandoned. Not even dynamite could blast her free. Two winters the *Discovery* was wedged in the ice of McMurdo Sound.

Shackleton's memories of the *Discovery* expedition are still tinged with bitterness, but it's nothing to do with the ship or the ice; only his own failure to achieve greatness. Determined to move beyond these frustrations once and for all, Shackleton will not give up his most ambitious expedition over the threat posed by ice.

'Come on, Frank,' he says. 'Let's be optimistic.'

Frank Wild cannot help but think of his brother, Ernie, on the other side of Antarctica. He is among the men known collectively as the Ross Sea Party who are responsible for laying supply depots to facilitate the second half of Shackleton's Antarctic crossing. With no communications possible between the two teams, they will have no idea that the expedition is so delayed.

There's a lot of grumbling and not much optimism from the crew. For eager adventure-seekers, a month in South Georgia seems a long time to wait. The sledge dogs, on the other hand, seem perfectly content to be taken off ship and housed on dry land, where the stench hangs in the air so thickly that even the wind can't shift it. Sometimes one of them escapes his chains and harasses the Grytviken pigs that roam free, snuffling greedily through slack and slimy drifts of whale waste.

After loading the extra stores and winter clothing, Shackleton's men must find other amusements to occupy their time. Frank Hurley has his camera out and is keen to explore. It's not long before he and Captain Worsley are scrambling up the hillside behind the settlement for a better view. They assess the mess of the whaling station below them and the dimpled expanse of slate-coloured water in the bay. Further around the coast there are the other whaling settlements of Husvik and Stromness, but apart from that, there is nothing but empty ocean for miles around. The interior of the island appears even more desolate – just a jumble of craggy, snow-covered peaks. Neither man is tempted to go further. Nobody has ever crossed South Georgia and they can see why.

There are other things to gladden the photographer's eye. Beyond the squalor of Grytviken, South Georgia brims with exotic sights – beaches thick with penguins, jousting sea elephants and countless nesting albatrosses. There's always an obliging whaling captain who'll take a boatload of visitors to secluded coastal spots to watch seals frolic and glaciers crumble into the sea like brittle white candy.

Over the course of weeks, new friendships are forged and evenings are spent in raucous enjoyment as they all chip away at the language barrier. Everyone loves the Norwegian folk songs, the jokes that need no translating. Soon enough photographs are passed around. The same words echo through the group – *these are my children at home, this is my wife back in Norway*. Some men simply shrug and say they are married to the sea. Suddenly the odours of the whaling settlement don't seem so offensive, the shoreline heaped with entrails so vile.

'Funny what a human being can get used to,' remarks Thomas Orde-Lees.

Orde-Lees himself has had a great deal to get used to since leaving Buenos Aires. Despite being a Royal Marine, and the strongest man by a long stretch, he finds himself at odds with shipboard life. The others have taken to calling him 'the Colonel', and not as a sign of respect. It's his exaggerated sense of importance that riles most. He says pulling on the tarry ropes makes his hands sore; he complains about scrubbing the decks when everyone spits on them; he refuses to eat beside Chippy, who he says is 'a perfect pig in every way', and blames his crippling seasickness on the size of the ship.

'I've never been sick on a man-o'-war,' he says grandly.

Once they get to Antarctica, he'll be busy with the expedition's motor sledges. Until then, Orde-Lees has nothing to do but jangle everyone's nerves. Sensing potential conflict, the Boss has come up with the perfect job for him: official stores-keeper. He'll spend his days on his own in the hold, fussing over cases of flour and powdered milk, jams and condiments, drawing up lists in a ledger and ticking away with a pencil to his heart's content.

Of course, as soon as Orde-Lees sets about restoring order to the stores below deck, his griping starts up. He's furious to find that men have been opening provision cases marked 'Shore' when they should only be using those marked 'Ship'.

'Those layabouts, grabbing whatever is within easy reach. Can't they read?' he fumes.

Even their former cook, the man fired in Buenos Aires, gets a telling-off.

'Reckless fool!' Orde-Lees shouts as if the man were still there. 'You've used up all the Worcestershire sauce!'

Rowing ashore one last time, Hurley appreciates the stillness of the December evening. Once the factories fall silent and the wind dies down, it's a peaceful place, even with the echo of dogs fighting on the hillside. He won't exactly miss Grytviken; certainly not the smell. But they have made some good friends among the whalers – honest, generous and rowdy men, who know how to throw a good party. He will miss them when the *Endurance* finally sets sail in the morning. Tonight will be a fond farewell.

Muck bobs about in the shallows as Hurley pulls the rowboat up the slipway beside a partly butchered whale. It's not immediately apparent in the dim light, but with the enormous beast to his left and waist-deep guts and gunge in every other direction, he realises he's hemmed in. Easy enough to climb over the whale using the ladder that somebody has left propped against the carcass. The rungs are greasy with blubber and as soon as he's on top, he's sliding. There is just enough time to cry out in alarm before everything goes dark.

Hurley doesn't know if he's sitting or floating, but he does know he's in the whale's rotten core. The air is thick and foul and coats the inside of his mouth. He imagines it clogging his lungs. Perhaps he will suffocate. He shouts, then vomits, shouts again. Dogs are barking somewhere. If he can hear them, then it's worth making more noise. Hurley yells like a madman. By some miracle, two Norwegians hear him. Despite being almost helpless with laughter, they manage to haul poor Hurley free. Head to toe, he's a mess. There'll be no party for Hurley this night but he has certainly had a Grytviken farewell to remember.

Shackleton has said his farewells ashore. His final evening in South Georgia is to be spent aboard the ship in his cabin, writing letters home. His wife, Emily, will not be so surprised to hear that their plans have gone awry, but she won't be pleased. He expected to be gone a year, but now it will be longer – quite a bit longer. When he's finished addressing the envelopes, he opens his diary to write up his last entry before they leave the world behind. As is often the case, he finds a poet's words sum up his emotions best. He takes St John Lucas's lines and reworks them, giving the poem 'The Ship of Fools' his own peculiar spin:

> *The world where wise men sit at ease,*
> *Fades from my unregretful eyes*
> *And blind across uncharted seas*
> *We stagger on our Enterprise.*

Hope and trepidation is what he feels on 5 December 1914. Tribulation is where he is heading.

CHAPTER THREE

WEDDELL SEA, SUMMER 1915

Captain Worsley is anxious. Gone is his natural exuberance, his happy-go-lucky attitude. Twenty-five years at sea has not prepared him for the stress of sailing in sub-Antarctic waters. The Weddell Sea is a navigator's nightmare. Keeping clear of icebergs is relatively easy – they're big, white, visible even at night; what keeps the captain awake is the thought of growlers, the razor-sharp chunks of ice that could easily slice through the hull.

Fortunately, Worsley is not the only one scanning the waves. Shackleton has stationed men on the bow and atop the mast. Nobody uses binoculars. Peripheral vision is far more effective on the open sea. The Boss admires Worsley's nerves of steel, but he himself is nervous. Suddenly the *Endurance* seems a rather fragile vessel.

The Weddell Sea turns out to be much more difficult to navigate than the Ross Sea. Will they ever reach Vahsel Bay? With each passing day he wonders how they'll get to the continent through this white labyrinth – a million square miles of it.

Whale meat swings back and forth in the rigging. The sledge dogs snatch at the frozen slabs, driven half mad with the sight of so much food hanging just out of reach. The cold has made them ravenous and snappy. A fair number remain in their kennels, out of sorts, after having picked up intestinal worms from eating rats in South Georgia. One dog has already been shot. Others may follow. With any luck, they've left the rats behind, but there's a cat on the ship and the hungrier dogs would happily tear it apart if given the chance. Not surprisingly, Mrs Chippy hasn't been seen on deck in weeks, preferring the warmth of the galley to the wind and sleet of the open seas. The cat is getting quite fat with all the love and attention lavished on him by the cook and his new helper, Perce Blackborow.

The young stowaway has taken to his new surroundings with a mix of awe and excitement. Everything is new and dramatic – the icebergs, the humpback whales glimpsed off the bow, the penguins that are seen in ever greater numbers as the ship forges a path through the tightening puzzle of ice floes. The new job he approaches with a bit more apprehension. He's never done much cooking for himself and here he is preparing three meals a day for twenty-eight men. Blackborow likes working with Green and has grown used to his high-pitched voice, which is apparently the result of losing a testicle in a dreadful accident. Perhaps one day he will ask Green if the rumours are true. Some of the men call him 'Doughballs', but never to his face. Blackborow refuses to laugh with them. It feels disloyal when Green has shown him nothing but kindness.

Most of the crew have forgotten how Blackborow came to be aboard and accept him as one of their own. Certainly, the slaps on the back at New Year as he helped Green serve up the ale and plum pudding made him feel like one of the lads. He's pleased the old salts don't mind responding to his endless questions, even when they don't know the answers. Even when he can tell they're making fun of him.

'Has anyone managed to break through all this pack ice to reach Antarctica?' he asks.

'Of course, lad. People do it all the time!'

More laughter.

'Who's done it?'

'Well, the Germans. They did it.'

Someone says: 'Yeah, they set out to do what we're doing.'

'Mad bastards.'

'What's funny?'

'Oh no, it ain't funny, lad. Filchner and his men got caught in the ice. Eight months they were stuck in the pack ice. Ended up drifting all the way back north. They got spat out of the Weddell Sea pretty much where we entered it.'

'All that wasted effort,' Blackborow says.

'Like I said, mad bastards.'

'Them?'

'No, us.'

Sometimes the *Endurance* proceeds under steam; sometimes Worsley abandons his southerly heading and steers the ship east or west in search of openings that will lead them to breaks in the otherwise resolutely frozen surface. Sometimes his tenacity is rewarded with a day or two of trouble-free navigating that nobody dares mention in case their lucky streak comes to an end. Other days they have no choice but to use the *Endurance* as a gigantic wedge, driven at half-speed into ice several feet thick to force their own path. Worsley thrills in charging the pack, riding the ship's cutwater up onto the ice edge and cleaving into its thick surface. The ice-breaking ability of the steel-sheathed bow is considerable, but the stern is vulnerable. The propeller and the rudder must be protected at all costs; any damage would be fiendishly hard to fix in near-freezing waters. Nobody in their right mind would willingly take the plunge to carry out repairs.

In the early weeks of January, they enjoy a stretch of more than 150 kilometres of open water. Finally, land comes into view. It's a mere 30 kilometres off in the distance. Shackleton names it the Caird Coast after an expedition sponsor. But there's nowhere to land. For five days straight they follow a 300-metre ice cliff to the west, hoping to get men and supplies ashore. When they finally come across a break in the barrier, a place they christen Glacier Bay, Worsley and others suggest they seize the opportunity. The Boss remains unconvinced.

'Let's continue to Vahsel Bay,' he says. 'If we land men here, we'll be adding another 200 kilometres to the overland journey.'

Worsley has come to appreciate Shackleton's judgement, his regard for the men. But is it cautiousness that governs this decision? Maybe he's being rash. Assuming no major obstacles lie in their way and their coal reserves last the distance, nobody's been ashore at Vahsel Bay, not even the German explorer Filchner, who gave it its name. Who knows what they'll find there? Back in London there are many people who consider this expedition a waste of money and potentially a risk to life and limb. London lies a long way off but as January wears on and still no landing spot presents itself, thoughts onboard the *Endurance* turn repeatedly to these naysayers. The captain is certainly one man who wonders if the Boss is pushing his luck.

'MR LAG'

IRELAND, 1882

Young Ernest Shackleton drives the spade into the ground and the weeds give way. An earthworm pays the price for the boy's enthusiasm, sliced in two before he realises what he's done. He watches with fascination and slight regret as the two halves squirm in confusion, finally effecting a sideways retreat into the tangle of grass beside the hole. The boy resumes his task, whistling. The South Pole, that's his goal. From 35 Marlborough Road, Dublin, Ernest plans to dig all the way through the centre of the earth. It must be possible. He's read about it in Jules Verne.

This is his father's spade, too heavy for a boy of eight. There's not much use for a spade in Dublin. It's been two years since they moved into town but Ernest still thinks about his boyhood home, the big house surrounded by fields. He remembers the openness that greeted him as he dashed through the front doors and into all that emerald countryside where adventure lay in every direction; the meadows, the woods and the stone towers of Kilkea Castle visible above the tall trees. Everything was worthy of investigation – a fallen nest with broken eggs, a hollow hedge to hide in, a swarm of ants to tempt onto a stick. There was no need to hurry; so he tarried. 'Mr Lag', the nanny called him.

Of course, Dublin suggests its own curiosities. He likes the bustle and grime of the city streets, following funeral processions and gangs of children, but the comings and goings on Marlborough Street alone are enough to keep a boy occupied from dawn to dusk. Today, it's the backyard of Number 35 where he's focusing his efforts and he's entirely alone. He'd like help with digging through the globe. The quantity of soil he has removed from the hole barely justifies the ache of his shoulders, the wobble in his skinny arms as he manoeuvres the spade up and down. That's not to say that he lacks resolve. There's sweat about his collar and his cheeks are red. There's progress. Fair testament to the family motto: By Endurance We Conquer.

Before long, the hole has attracted the maid. She glances out the window suspiciously, knowing she'll have to restore order in the garden once young Ernest loses interest. He waves to her to indicate that he has something to say. She raises the window sash.

'Can you help with this?'

'No. I'm busy.'

'Please, I'm getting so tired here in the sun.'

The maid slides the window shut in answer.

Ernest has another idea and sneaks back into the house. When he returns to the garden, he gives a few hearty digs then starts jumping from foot to foot and shouting. The maid appears on the back step, her neck craning to see what all the commotion is about. The other Shackleton children are already tumbling from the house to Ernest's cries of, 'Treasure! Treasure!'

The children bend to the hole. His older sister Alice looks bewildered but doesn't mention the fact that she recognises the treasure. Two years younger, Frank tries to jerk the spade from his brother's grasp.

'Look,' Ernest says to the maid. 'Someone wanted to hide their jewels.'

Her lips twitch, the hanging skin under her chin quivers. The maid's ardour with the spade is impressive given she's spent the morning traipsing up and down stairs hefting coal and fresh linen. But she clearly has plenty of energy for digging out treasure. The Shackleton children watch, fascinated.

'But I still don't understand,' says Alice finally, 'why was Mama's ring in the hole?'

The maid pauses. 'Very good, young Master Ernest, you've had your fun.'

The younger brother is overjoyed to finally have his turn with the spade. He takes to the task with the passion of one keen to prove his worth. Ernest doesn't stop him. He realises that getting to the South Pole is going to take much more effort. And there's sure to be a better way than this.

CHAPTER FOUR

WEDDELL SEA, AUTUMN, WINTER 1915

Should we concede defeat? wonders Shackleton after yet another week of drifting with the ice. February is over. The southern summer is coming to an end and they're not even drifting in the right direction. Is this really the end of his grand plan to be the first to cross Antarctica? Conferring with Worsley and Wild, the Boss realises he's out of options. It's a depressing thought. If only they had hurried ashore at Glacier Bay when they had the chance. Fortunately, Worsley is not one to say, *I told you so.*

Instead, the captain says, 'Blasted nor-easterly. It's

shifted all the ice in the Weddell Sea hard up against the land and here we are in the thick of it.'

One would never guess that the ship is afloat on an ocean. There's not a hint of swell or open water. For a time, they considered casting out for the coast on sledges, but what lies between them and land could only be described as an obstacle course. Hummocks and pressure ridges rise from the frozen surface like convoluted conversations between ice floes. It might be feasible for a man scrambling on hands and knees to get through, but it's an impossible proposition for dogs and sledges burdened with hundreds of kilos of gear.

'Maybe a good strong southerly could break up all this mess,' Frank Wild suggests.

'I think we need to face facts . . .' Worsley pauses. He doesn't want to be the first to say it.

'We're trapped like an almond in the middle of a chocolate bar,' says Thomas Orde-Lees, walking past their huddle on the deck. Nobody ever asks his opinion, but after months in the cramped confines of the *Endurance*, they're used to hearing it.

The Boss sighs. 'We'll reassess our options in the spring.'

Shackleton is becoming something of an expert in deferred dreams. The number of times he has had to swallow his pride or shelve his plans would make most folk avoid commitments of any sort. After taking part in

34

Scott's *Discovery* expedition in 1902 and his own *Nimrod* expedition in 1907, Shackleton should have left Antarctica shaking his fist and uttering a curse. And yet, twice he left this land of profound disappointment plotting his return. His wife finds it baffling how somebody could be so bruised by a place and still go back for more of a thrashing.

To be fair, it wasn't a complete failure. During *Nimrod*, Shackleton had got further south with Frank Wild and two others than he had with Scott and Wilson during *Discovery*. Of course, Roald Amundsen had smashed all their records in 1912, ending the game once and for all.

'A man must shape himself to a new mark directly the old one goes to ground,' Shackleton tells the assembled men as their new plan is laid out. They must transform the ship into winter quarters. With any luck, when spring arrives, they will be able to get ashore and resume their adventure. There is every reason to believe the Ross Sea party will have fulfilled their depot-laying obligations, so there will be no impediment to achieving their aim. Inspiring words, but nobody can ignore a million tonnes of ice pressing against the ship. Nor the strange new sounds that emanate from the ice fields.

Stores must be rearranged, sleeping arrangements improved, heating rigged up to withstand winter's low temperatures. There is so much to keep the men busy that few have time or the energy to ponder the many challenges the next few months must surely hold.

Doctors Macklin and McIlroy discuss diet with Shackleton. Scurvy is their main concern. Shackleton agrees. He's suffered the effects of the debilitating condition and knows it can be fatal if not treated. Each man must receive a generous portion of fresh meat as a preventative measure. Hunting parties are sent out amid the tall ice hummocks with Captain Worsley directing from the masthead with signal flags. The Weddell seals are quite disgusting, with their foaming snotty faces and meat that often appears diseased or unappetising. The crab-eater seals are far more appealing and often carry undigested fish in their bellies – a delicacy, if one can set aside thoughts of where it came from. Getting the seal carcasses back to the ship is a tricky business and usually requires four or five men to get the job done quickly. Left too long in the cold, the carcasses solidify. All the Antarctic old-timers know it is better to butcher the meat while the flesh is still warm. Poor Blackborow is learning the hard way, and discovering the agony of frostbitten fingers. He's still too slow at cutting up the seal carcasses, although he can now skin and gut a penguin in double-quick time.

Much of the meat and offal is fed to the dogs. Another fifteen have had to be destroyed since the *Endurance* got stuck. Macklin and McIlroy perform the post-mortems and concur: it's the intestinal worms again. Moving them off the ship seems wise. There'll be more room, less likelihood of the infection spreading. Igloos or dogloos, as someone suggests they should be called, spring up around the ship. There's a fair bit of debate around the best design and the process soon turns competitive. Before long, turrets and other architectural flourishes are added. Nothing a dog would notice, but the photographer is certainly happy to snap away while there is still adequate natural light to capture the scene.

Four young puppies will stay aboard with the Irishman Tom Crean. Judging by his weathered face and taciturn disposition, he seems an unlikely mother. Lavishing tenderness on puppies seems unlikely behaviour for a hardened polar veteran. Tom Crean doesn't say much about his experiences with Captain Scott's ill-fated *Terra Nova* expedition or about the two medals King George awarded him for valour. Men like Crean never tell anecdotes about dead national heroes or crow about their own brave deeds. And despite having a lot to say, he is completely silent on the subject of saving other men's lives.

As the evenings draw out and autumn gives way to winter, card games become an even more popular pastime. Poker chips are improvised from whale bones, a gift from the Norwegians in South Georgia – the same men who warned them about the ice in the Weddell Sea. The irony is not lost on Shackleton, Worsley and Wild, as they wage their poker war with Chippy and Tom Crean on the wardroom table. No money changes hands in the ebb and flow of reversing fortunes. Each man wins a round and then loses his shirt in the next.

Worsley loses a lot more than anyone else and accepts a dare to clear his debts. With a great deal of whooping the captain runs barefoot down the gangplank and drives headfirst, and completely naked, into the snow. It's the first wash he has had in a very long time and he makes a show of it for the observers cheering him on from the deck. He calls to them by name, inviting them to join him as he rolls about in the drift. There are more than a few smelly men aboard who would benefit from an exhilarating snow bath, but the mere thought of taking their layers off in minus 20 is torture enough.

CHAPTER FIVE

WEDDELL SEA, SPRING 1915

The radio is dead. Static is all they pick up over the winter months. Transmitting a message, alerting people to their plight, would be a futile exercise in any case. What could be done? Nobody can help them; the *Endurance* is icebound and unreachable. Of course, it would be a relief if their families could be reassured of their safety. Their safety! They feel bad even mentioning the word in the context of their situation. They are warm and well-fed in the Weddell Sea; meanwhile a world war is raging in Europe.

The war effort is discussed at mealtimes and in the

bunks at night. Nobody has any idea what's happening. They assume that war is still raging but it's all speculation. There are a few raised voices at times. Being without news for so long is frustrating, but the thought of not participating is worse. The lives of brothers, cousins, friends are being sacrificed while their days are filled with carefree pursuits – reading, card games, betting squares of chocolate and packets of cigarettes on the outcome of sledge races, playing hockey and football on the ice floes in the moonlight.

The Boss likes to remind the men that, before leaving England, he had offered to put the expedition and all its resources at the Royal Navy's disposal, but that he had received a telegram from the Admiralty that simply read: *Proceed.* There will undoubtedly be criticism in the British press on his return, of him personally, of his failed expedition, of him stealing away so many young men during a time of national crisis. But there are also many on board the *Endurance* who believe strongly that they should be on the battlefield rather than drifting aimlessly in the frozen wastes. He can't blame them. He too wishes that he was living a life of action and not wasting his time.

The scientists have plenty of books to read but very little room to carry out any practical science when harsh conditions keep them below deck for much of the time. Leonard Hussey, the meteorologist, is happy out in the open whatever the weather – even during the dark days of winter.

Ice storms, blizzards, katabatic winds have been fascinating to experience firsthand, and even on calm days, a schedule of atmospheric readings has kept him busy.

The biologist Robert Clark has also been able to carry on with his work, even if his penguin dissections on the wardroom table are not to everyone's liking. It's been a struggle for James Wordie, the geologist, to use his time meaningfully. The only rock samples he's come across out in the middle of a frozen sea are those he finds wedged in icebergs or piled in the stomachs of Clark's dissected penguins. While he hopes eventually to set foot on the continent, nothing is certain. At worst it will be a frustrating gap in his university career.

His colleague from Cambridge, Reginald James, or 'Jimmy' as everyone calls him, is in a similar position. The bespectacled physicist would love to be collecting data but instead finds himself spending more and more time with his head in the *Encyclopædia Britannica* or constructing elaborate scientific instruments out of old biscuit tins. Professionally, the year is ruined.

The return of the sun after three months of winter darkness brings renewed hope. Daylight lifts morale; they'll be able to spend more time outdoors, but only warmer temperatures will end their plight. Since it was beset, the ship has drifted more than 600 kilometres from the shores of the continent.

To the men it seems highly unlikely that the expedition will go ahead and every day of northward drift brings them closer to home, to seeing their loved ones again. But first the ice must release them, and so far, it shows no sign of doing that.

If anything, the ice's grip on the ship is tighter and the pressure exerted on her is building. It is as if the landscape has been dozing, and now it is awakening. The dogs are moved once again – not for everyone's comfort and convenience this time, but for the animals' own safety. It was relatively easy to ignore the hollow-sounding rumbles in the distance over winter. Now the discordant noises of grinding floes seem to be coming from just beyond the ship's railings.

It's enough to get Shackleton out of bed and pacing the decks, all the while thinking, *What the ice gets, it keeps.* Meanwhile Captain Worsley lies rigid with apprehension in his berth listening to the creaks and groans of the hull. Some of the more suspicious sailors have it in their heads that the pressure is worse whenever there's a record playing in the wardroom. A few of them have even expressed a desire to throw the gramophone overboard to avoid any further trouble. Understandably, there is vehement opposition to any action that would deprive them of one of their few sources of entertainment. Without the mental medicine of music, as the Boss calls it, they'd be utterly forlorn.

Imprisonment on the ship has been a struggle for everyone. They all rail against the tedium of days spent below deck in stale air and dimly lit cabins, but the boredom is perhaps worse for the sailors, who have virtually nothing to do. It's been torture for Walter How, Alf Cheetham and the superstitious old salt Thomas McLeod, who have been at sea since a young age. The American William Bakewell, and seamen like Ernest Holness and John Vincent, are used to the black water and strong winds of the North Sea. Vincent would gladly swap his life of comparative leisure aboard the *Endurance* for the hard physical labour of the trawling fleet. A sailor's everyday life has rhythm and purpose. Here on the Weddell Sea, a drink on Saturday night is all one can look forward to. And how they do!

The Boss makes no distinction between the blunt and bluff sailors and the more sophisticated men with university degrees. Everyone receives the same straightforward treatment and the same allocation of food and drink. Through sharing a laugh, the Boss feels like he's got the measure of most men and is keen to keep the atmosphere of the ship casual. That's not to say that all standards have been relaxed. When personal grooming takes a slide, he orders compulsory haircuts. Like a good leader, he is first to submit to the shears. Lewis Rickinson is the ship's engineer, not a barber, and by the time he's finished, the Boss looks a fright. Swapping seats with Shackleton, Rickinson ends up looking even worse. Over the course of the evening every man tries his hand at improving the appearance of his shipmates, and the Saturday night alcohol ration only makes matters worse.

'We all look like convicts,' says Chippy.

'Well, we might as well be in prison.' Worsley scratches his newly visible scalp where it's been nicked. 'We're all serving the same long sentence on this ship.'

Laughter repairs most of the damage. Each man looks as grim as the next. Finally, Hurley takes a group photograph and they all raise a toast.

'To our sweethearts and wives . . .'

'May they never see us like this!'

'. . . may they never meet!'

It's the usual lighthearted line but everyone laughs as if it's the first time they've heard it. Amid the rowdiness that ensues, Vincent sidles up to Perce Blackborow and smiles, 'Give me that, boy.'

Blackborow is at first confused. 'My drink?'

Vincent nods.

The young man does as he's told and tips his grog into the older man's mug. Last time he refused, thinking it was said in jest, Vincent knocked his supper onto the floor. A pecking order has emerged among the sailors. Blackborow has noticed how the other seamen stand back and allow Vincent first dibs whenever any luxuries are dished up. Nobody would call him a bully to his face, although there have been complaints made to Captain Worsley about

Vincent's heavy-handedness. He was demoted from his position as bosun long before their arrival in South Georgia, but it hasn't made much of a difference to his behaviour. He likes to strike when there's noise and bustle and his bullying is unlikely to be seen by others. Blackborow makes a mental note to stay well clear of him, on Saturday nights especially.

Later in the evening when the gramophone is set up on the wardroom table, there's a hideous cracking sound, loud enough to put an immediate stop to conversation. The music plays on, even as a terrible whine and shudder travels up through the ribs of the ship.

'Stop the music,' says the Boss.

The men's eyes travel around the room as they listen. Peculiar sounds have become all too familiar in recent times. Captain Worsley has described it like the snoring of a giant or an enormous train with squeaky axles being shunted with much bumping and clattering. To Frank Wild, it is like listening to distant London traffic while sitting in a city park. But this time it is different. These sounds are coming from the bowels of the ship, and there can be no mistake as to the cause; what they hear next is the cracking and splitting of timbers.

PART II

PATIENCE

CHAPTER SIX

OCTOBER 1915

'Just look at him,' mutters Vincent. 'Standing there like an idiot.' He dumps the crate onto the snow alongside the mountain of provision boxes, clothing, tents, scientific equipment and sledges. Abandoning ship is backbreaking work.

'You talking about our Cambridge genius?'

Vincent scoffs, 'He doesn't know his arse from his elbow.'

Hurley overhears the griping and can tell immediately who it is about. 'Jimmy!' he calls. 'I need your help over here with the dogs.'

Jimmy pushes his round glasses up his nose and gives his friend a wave but doesn't move from the spot on the ice floe.

'How can somebody so brainy be so stupid?' Vincent mumbles.

Vincent's humour is often mean-spirited and his jokes are rarely funny. But in this instance, the men are all in agreement. Jimmy may be a Cambridge-educated physicist, but he behaves like an imbecile when it comes to tackling any practical task. Too clumsy to be sent up the mast, a hopeless ditherer on deck, Jimmy has also proven himself ill-suited to even the most menial jobs, like carrying boxes. He's become famous for doing the daftest things. Asked to collect water during the sea journey, Jimmy tossed the bucket over the side then simply watched as the rope tied to the handle snaked its way across the deck and disappeared along with the precious bucket. Such a lack of common sense irritates the Boss and the captain and sends the sailors into a rage, as it is generally up to them to fix his blunders. Even his fellow scientists find his eccentric ways testing and remain baffled by his awkward attempts to entertain the more uneducated crewmembers with intellectual word games or pompous scientific soliloquys. All of this makes the close friendship he has struck up with Hurley the photographer the biggest mystery of them all.

Jimmy starts to walk towards where Hurley is organising the dogs, then stops and looks about as if he has entirely forgotten where he is and what he should be doing. The situation is far from confusing. Everyone else is offloading cargo from the stricken ship. Everyone understands the need for speed. Jimmy just seems lost. Hurley looks at him and laughs. Jimmy doesn't represent another pair of hands, just another thing to be managed; easier ignored at a time like this than deployed.

Another eccentric left to his own devices is Orde-Lees. Amid the bustle of unloading the *Endurance*, he's doing the rounds of the immediate area, picking up any interesting bits and pieces that have been dropped or thrown away. He's fond of scrounging and has a large collection of nails, string, broken glass and lengths of rope. In the past Orde-Lees has collected up discarded seal heads to boil down in a pot in the galley, much to the cook's chagrin. He has quite a collection of souvenir jawbones that he hoped to sell back in Britain on his return, but all of it will stay aboard the *Endurance* in the cabin he has shared with Jimmy for the past nine months.

Aside from their eccentricities and a tendency towards seasickness, Orde-Lees and Jimmy don't have much in common. During their months of confinement there have been the usual disagreements about snoring and mess. According to Orde-Lees, Jimmy doesn't pull his weight when it comes doing his portion of the housework. For months he's accused the physicist of 'hanging' his clothes on the floor and wiping his feet on Orde-Lees's lower bunk before hopping into bed. Perhaps the bickering between the two men will finally cease. Tents are their new accommodations and bunks are a thing of the past.

The dogs are moved once again onto the ice floe. Down a canvas slide they zip, some sideways, some tumbling on top of other dogs as they bounce over the ice. Tom Crean thinks it best to carry his four puppies down the gangplank and avoid the carnage. Fights are breaking out constantly. Hurley grabs one dog by its harness and kicks another free while Dr Macklin uses a whip to separate two of the larger dogs. Left alone, they'll tear each other to pieces as well as anyone that gets in the way. Macklin has already been bitten on the arm. Some of these creatures weigh 50 or 60 kilos and have energy to burn. Soon enough they'll be hitched to the sledges and put to work. The puppies won't, however. Even though Tom Crean started training them up in the harness over the winter, they are still too young to be of any real use. Crean is aware that his puppies won't be going much further; sadly their days are numbered.

The dogs are picketed on steel lines, away from the tents where the men will sleep. They don't like being tied up but it's necessary when feeding time comes so they neither savage the men nor their fellow dogs. Ripping into the seal meat, the dogs barely register the penguins that waddle into view. Eight emperors are an impressive sight. Any other day, they'd be clubbed and butchered for meat, but everyone is too exhausted to do anything but admire their stately waddling. Like a delegation of Antarctic dignitaries, they approach the *Endurance*, tip their heads back and start up an eerie wailing. Even the dogs turn from their feast and stare as their singing rises to a haunting vibrato. It's a short episode but it has a chilling effect.

'It's a bad omen,' says superstitious McLeod. 'None of us will get back to our homes again.'

Most of the other men are too busy for omens, although they're trying not to think about the grim situation. The floes pile against the sides of the ship like a slow-motion wave hitting her broadside. In some places, spikes of ice have penetrated the outer sheathing. The ship won't sink yet. Even though many planks have popped and rivulets of salt water run down the inside of her hull, the ship is held tight, braced by the same destructive forces that are crushing her sides. Chippy has constructed a coffer dam. He hopes it will hold the water back long enough for most of the vital equipment and supplies to be offloaded.

'It's only temporary,' he says repeatedly, perhaps fearing that he'll get the blame when the ship sinks.

After months of being harassed, the *Endurance* is finally giving up the fight. The rudder is gone, her ribs are broken. At one stage, the ship was heaved several metres above the line of the floe and tipped on her beams. It happened so suddenly that the cook had to grab a hefty pot of stew off the stove and hold it aloft until Blackborow came to his aid. Thankfully, the ice eventually relaxed the ship back down to its original position. Dinner was saved but nerves were rattled.

Shackleton feels sick when he sees the buckled steel plating in the engine room floor; it's the clearest indication yet of the forces they're up against. He's cleared his cabin; anything left behind is surplus to requirements. It was hard to decide which books to take, which to abandon. He'll miss the volumes of poetry that have added so much to his winter evenings. Much of it is committed to memory, however, so in a sense, it is not lost. Coleridge has been circling in his head since morning; the beautiful line from the 'Ancient Mariner' about it growing *wondrous cold and ice, mast-high, came floating by*. The framed Kipling will need to be saved. He takes it off the wall and removes the backing. The poem 'If' has always been a source of inspiration. He reads it over, before folding it into his pocket.

The air is bracing on the slippery deck. Shackleton grasps the ice-covered rigging with one hand, hails Wild with the other. They share a smoke and a smile. There's a joke for Worsley too as the captain directs traffic down the gangplank.

The Boss has a plan. They'll try to get to Paulet Island, where the Swedish explorer Nordenskjöld and his crew left a cache of supplies twelve years earlier. Like the *Endurance*, their ship had been abandoned. The Swedes had survived their ordeal, even though they had to wait two years to be rescued. Their story is heartening in some ways, sobering in others. One aspect that worries Shackleton is that the Swedes only had to travel 25 kilometres to Paulet Island. He and his crew face a journey of 550 kilometres to reach salvation.

Whistling a tune to steady his nerves, Green prepares what will be their last meal onboard the ship. A nervous laugh escapes whenever he hears the hull's deep groan. After the day's exertions the men will need a good feed. The smell of penguin in beef dripping brings Mrs Chippy to the galley. The cat stares up at Green and yowls in a way that usually results in a morsel dropping to the galley floor. Green offers a cube of the penguin liver he's cooking up with bacon – a treat for men whose morale might need a boost.

'Blackborow, ring the dinner bell,' Green says. 'Grub's up.'

Blackborow wonders what the evening meal will look like tomorrow. Camp kitchen – that is what Green has been calling the place where they'll prepare three meals a day for twenty-eight men.

'That'll be brilliant for the camp kitchen . . . When we're in the camp kitchen, we'll need to do it this way . . .'

Green makes it sounds exciting, like they're about to embark on an adventure in the wilderness. Blackborow won't waste time worrying about what the future holds. Besides, he's heard some of the men say they'll be home by Christmas.

'MICK'

LONDON 1888

His Irish accent doesn't belong in London. At school they call him 'Mick'. On St Patrick's Day they make him fight the other Irish boy. Everybody shouting and laughing, egging them on and kicking them like dogs. He doesn't like it. Before the family moved here from Dublin, his parents spent a fair amount of money getting him to sound more English, less Mick. After the effort and expense, a lilt is all that remains of Ernest's Irish brogue. It's not much but it's enough of a difference to get the boys of Fir Lodge Prep School laughing. The name sticks. Eventually he's happy as Mick, sometimes Mickey, never Ernest. Unless it's family.

Mick Shackleton gets on fine at Dulwich College. He's not a rabble-rouser, or a great sportsman. He's too reflective for that, but he's not a scholar either. The masters despair of him, assume he won't amount to much. Poetry, on the other hand. Now there's a pure pleasure. He can quote it 'by the yard'. He's been brought up with the greats. Tennyson at the dinner table. Now he recites Longfellow in the school halls, Campbell's 'Ye Mariners of England' to whoever will listen – the lines spring from his lips as if written for him alone.

There's poetry in the sea too. It calls to him on his days off school, the times when he plays truant, leading a few others astray. They beetle along shorelines, ramble in a group on the wharves, look from the bridges over the mighty Thames. Perhaps he'll join the navy. Ernest knows his father can't afford the training. Not on a doctor's salary. But the merchant navy . . . perhaps that's the career.

The tramp steamer captain seems a friendly chap. Up for dockside conversation.

'I'm a hard worker and a quick learner,' Ernest declares with force.

'Of course you are,' replies the tramp steamer captain. 'But you're too young.'

Ernest sighs. He supposes it's just as well. He can't yet swim.

CHAPTER SEVEN

OCTOBER 1915

A sombre atmosphere is to be expected after supper on 27 October. The scene on the ice floe is chaotic and it's fearfully cold. Meteorologist Hussey says the thermometer reads minus 26 degrees. Each man has been allocated extra winter clothing and half a kilo of tobacco. They would all love to slip into a fur-lined sleeping bag on this bare-bones miserable night, but there are not enough for everyone. Ten men will miss out. Drawing lots seems the only fair thing to do, although Shackleton, Wild and Tom Crean all opt out on the spot. Having endured freezing temperatures many times before, they feel they're more mentally prepared to make do with blankets.

The *Endurance* hangs back in the twilight, suddenly an ugly, broken thing. Hurley sizes the ship up from different angles and focuses his pocket camera. It's almost indecent to be watching with such a cool eye the death throes of their dear ship, their home, their only link with the outside world. A photographer must have a steady hand and he must be prepared to capture the moment, however despairing he feels. Almost all of his equipment remains aboard; it's simply too cumbersome to bring. His heart aches at the thought of the cinema film, double-packed into tins, sealed and soldered to protect the fragile footage. As for the precious negatives – a whole year's worth of work, more than 550 glass plates – salvaging that must surely be a priority. But he has no idea how to transport such heavy stuff. To save it all, he'd need the cavalry.

Shackleton is the last to leave the *Endurance* that day. They won't sleep or eat aboard the ship again. He strides down the gangplank rubbing his hands energetically, as if impatient to embark on the next stage of the journey. He joins Frank Wild on the floe. Nobody would notice the look that passes between them, but the two old friends understand each other immediately. The situation is as bad as it could be. But what should the Boss tell the assembled crew?

'Our current position is 69 degrees south. The ocean currents are sending our floe due north. We've already drifted from 76 degrees south. That's 7 degrees of latitude.'

A few muted cheers echo around the group. The Boss holds up his hands, keen to arrest any false hope. He can already see where the men's thoughts might take them.

'We're heading in the right direction,' someone calls out. 'What if we did absolutely nothing, just waited things out?'

'Well, we would eventually find ourselves on the doorstep of the South Atlantic. Not good.'

There's agreement. It's a large area of treacherous and empty ocean, too: no islands, virtually no shipping.

Shackleton continues, 'We need to head in a more westerly direction. You've all heard me mention Paulet Island. That's a good start. We'll find shelter and food . . .'

'. . . and solid ground,' comes a helpful suggestion from one of the seamen.

'Indeed,' says Shackleton. 'Worsley has calculated the distance.'

Worsley nods. 'It's just over 500 kilometres. As the crow flies.'

'How soon before anyone's going to come looking for us?' asks Green.

Shackleton clears his throat, but he doesn't spare the truth. 'Nobody is expecting to see us until February 1916. Three months from now.'

'Will they know where to start looking?' Blackborow asks.

The Boss shakes his head. 'That's the other thing. Nobody knows where we are. They'd all assume that we're on the Antarctic continent.'

'But we're not,' says Vincent rather redundantly.

'Don't forget there's a war on,' grumbles Chippy. 'Nobody's going to be worried about us when they have the hands full.'

The men stand around, thinking the whole thing through, chatting about the best way forward, but no matter how they approach their dilemma, the conclusion is the same.

'We're going to have to rescue ourselves, aren't we?' Jimmy says to Hurley. For once he's got it right.

Worsley doesn't like the idea of only taking two lifeboats. With twenty-eight men, they'll need all three to make the ocean crossing to Paulet Island. How they'll drag the boats over the tortured pack ice without damaging them is another concern. Turbulent seas have nothing on the jagged towers and fortresses of ice that lie in their path. If it was up to him, he would establish a camp on a solid flat iceberg and wait it out. If the boats are compromised, so is their survival. He's tried to talk Shackleton around to his way of thinking, to no avail. The Boss is impatient and convinced that, in order to maintain discipline and order, the men need to focus on achieving an objective, even a doubtful one.

Turning in for the night, the men indulge in idle chat in the tents. There are five in total, pitched 100 metres from the ship. Sleeping arrangements have been thought through carefully. The Boss's primary objective is to separate the troublemakers. Conflict must be avoided at all cost, even if that means making the ultimate sacrifice of having the most wearying company in his own tent. Wild has also volunteered to take his share. Poor Worsley has drawn the short straw and ended up with Orde-Lees.

He's every bit as exhausted as his men, but the Boss doesn't sleep; he paces about their new camp in the half-light, wondering what feats of endurance will be required to get everyone home safely. The dogs raise their heads as he passes by. A few offer a wag of the tail. *Poor creature, you have no idea*, he thinks. Death is the best they can hope for now. What a dreadful task it will be to have to destroy these fine animals once they have fulfilled their purpose of pulling sledges across the ice to a place where they can launch the boats. They cannot be taken on board, of course. Nor left on the floe to fend for themselves.

With a head so full of regrets, the Boss doesn't notice the jagged line that cuts across the ice in front of him until he almost falls into it.

'Get up! Get up! The ice is breaking up!'

Within seconds the crack has widened to several inches. It snakes through the camp like a lit fuse. Now Frank Wild is flinging open tent flaps and shouting too.

Those who are first out register horror. The crack in the ice floe passes right under one of the tents. Some of the men struggle into clothing and boots, some haul their belongings into the open. Not all the tents lie in harm's way, but everything will need to be moved to a safer area. Shackleton points to a larger floe with no outward signs of disturbance. The men drag heavy crates free of danger, somehow finding superhuman strength despite their day-time exertions.

'For goodness' sake, save the Heinz!' screams Orde-Lees.

By one o'clock in the morning the tents are pitched again and the men lie down, although most are too agitated to find sleep. Wild remains with the Boss and spends the rest of the night keeping watch for more cracks. By five o'clock the light is improving and it's not such a strain on the eyes. They both wonder why one tent lies heaped on the snow, the canvas stiff with cold. The Boss nudges it with his foot and a head appears along with clouds of white breath and a beard covered with frost.

'I'm bloody frozen.'

'What are you doing, Hurley?'

'The others joined the other tent. I couldn't get this tent sorted on my own.'

Shackleton and Wild untangle the photographer from complicated layers of icy canvas. His feet, his shoulders, his hands feel dead with cold.

'We all need a hot drink,' Shackleton suggests.

Hurley nods enthusiastically and shoves his hands into his armpits.

'I'm not fiddling with that blubber stove,' says Wild. 'Not with freezing hands. Let's get some petrol from the ship and light that.'

Fortunately, the milk powder is found in one of the first provision boxes they open. The case of petrol burns ferociously in the dawn light. Greedy for the heat, they toast their hands and turn to warm their backsides in the generous blaze. By seven o'clock there's a five-gallon drum of hot milk.

'Let's take hot drinks around the tents,' says the Boss. 'It will give the lads a boost after last night.'

The steaming milk is a welcome sight. There are those who still grumble about being cold, about sleeping on the hard-packed snow. A few seem reluctant to show much appreciation. Wild can't help but show his irritation.

'If any of you gentlemen would like your boots cleaned just put them outside!' he snaps.

The milk is barely lukewarm by the time it reaches Wild and Shackleton's lips.

'Almost seven years to the day,' Wild says. 'You and I, we were setting out on the great southern journey with our ponies.'

Shackleton grins. 'Do you remember poor Adams? One day into the journey and that pony kicked him in the shins.'

'Ach, yes,' Wild winces at the recollection, 'and you could see the bone.'

'He wouldn't turn back,' Shackleton sighs. 'He acted as if nothing had happened!'

'Adams wasn't such a great manhauler though, was he? Neither was Marshall. We should have taken others in their place. We might have made it to the South Pole instead of turning back.' Wild sips his milk thoughtfully.

Shackleton shrugs. 'Better a live donkey than a dead lion.'

Wild gives a bitter laugh. 'Do you remember my lucky escape? When poor Socks plunged down the crevasse on the Beardmore Glacier? He almost took me with him. How can a pony disappear without a trace?'

'One second there, but the next, nothing but a hole six feet wide. And you with your hand round the rein too,' reminds the Boss.

'Gave me a nasty jerk but my glove was loose. It just flew off and down the hole it went. After the poor pony.' Wild gives a chuckle. 'Do you know what my first thought was?'

'What?'

'Thank goodness I won't have to shoot Socks.'

Shackleton roars with laughter. 'You'd have had to! That horrible maze of crevasses we arrived at afterwards.

You couldn't lead a pony through that. There wasn't even a patch solid enough to pitch a tent.'

Wild and Shackleton slip into a companionable silence. Between them, they've suffered every trial and indignity the continent has to offer: hunger, exhaustion, diarrhoea from eating spoiled pony meat, chafed thighs, windburnt faces, parched mouths and scabby lips.

Wild still recalls how his hands were so badly blistered from cold, it looked like he was carrying a handful of black grapes. 'Do you remember what I said to you about never coming back here?'

'Yes,' says Shackleton. 'We all say silly things like that at one time or another.'

Wild shakes his head.

'Orde-Lees said a funny thing to me as I was leaving the ship,' Shackleton says suddenly. 'That I should be glad the ship was lost. That I needed something exciting to happen in the book I'm going to write about our adventure.'

'Orde-Lees,' Wild chuckles. 'What a strange fellow! Though I suppose it's a good thing that he assumes we'll survive our ordeal and you'll write a book about it.'

After a pause, Shackleton says, 'We're going to have to shoot the dogs eventually.'

'I know,' says Wild.

'And poor old Mrs Chippy. But probably a lot sooner.'

CHAPTER EIGHT

OCTOBER 1915

Green's camp kitchen is a windy place. Preparing a meal in the lee of an overturned lifeboat propped up with broken oars is far from ideal. It's a new experience for both the cook and his young helper to cook over a blubber stove as well.

'Is the stove supposed to billow all this black stuff?' asks Blackborow as he stirs the pemmican hoosh. He tries to swerve out of the way whenever the heavy smoke wafts in his direction, but it is inescapable. Already his newly issued Burberry windbreaker has taken on an oily sheen and his eyes are burning.

Green gives a sad nod. 'How's the hoosh looking?'

'How's it supposed to look?'

'Soupy. Stewy.'

'Smells okay.'

It's the first time Blackborow has seen pemmican. Simple sledging food to be enjoyed on the move, Green said. Not that he's ever eaten it himself. It didn't look appetising when he unwrapped it. It looked like a brick. But they followed the instructions on the packet and the block of fat and dried meat eventually melted down into the boiling pot of water. Green told him there'd be biscuits too, but Blackborow was horrified when he saw them. They're nothing like the ones his grandma might bake. Nothing like shortbread. These biscuits are more like squares cut from a plywood box.

'Soak 'em in hoosh, you'll be mopping up the scraps,' says Green as he watches the young man eye the mound of biscuits with suspicion.

Blackborow sighs. He keeps expecting Mrs Chippy to come calling. It's sad. Chippy is angry with the Boss for killing the cat – or at least ordering its execution. But they couldn't possibly take the cat where they are heading. Besides, it wouldn't be long before the dogs got hold of it. Hurley spent all afternoon digging two big holes in the ice floe – one for the cat and Crean's poor dead puppies, the other for all the personal effects they must leave behind. They're only allowed a kilo per man on the journey. Everyone has agonised about what to take, what to toss in Hurley's hole. When a few men start to call the place 'Dump Camp', the name sticks.

'Take photos of your wives and sweethearts,' the Boss encouraged them.

Dr Macklin told everyone toilet paper was more useful.

Blackborow felt quite shocked at the sight of the Boss ripping pages from the Bible. Not just any Bible either, but Queen Alexandra's gift to the expedition. It landed with a real thud when he tossed it on top of all the odds and ends in the hole. Blackborow wonders if everything will eventually end up on the ocean floor when the ice floe drifts north and melts away to nothing. Funny to think of Queen Alexandra's Bible surrounded by fish, draped in seaweed.

The men gather to the comforting smells of food, keen to know what's for breakfast. They'll retreat to the tents to enjoy their first hot meal off-ship once it's ready. It's too cold to stand around in the open for long.

Blackborow would like to say something to Tom Crean, but he's a bit intimidated by him . He can never quite gauge the Irishman's mood. He's not bad-tempered or mean like Vincent. Often his deeply lined face appears thoughtful, especially when he's smoking his pipe. What's he thinking about? Blackborow would love to ask. Certainly, Tom Crean has many things to think about – his experiences on Captain Scott's expeditions, his rescue of Evans, how he marched for eighteen hours straight without food to get help, how it felt to float out to sea on an ice floe. All of these stories Blackborow has heard third-hand. One thing is clear: Crean doesn't mention his medals. Blackborow wonders, if he had them here, would he toss them into the hole with all the other precious yet useless things?

Hussey is delighted his banjo has been saved from the icy grave. It weighs over 10 kilos and the meteorologist was resigned to losing it. But the Boss grasped it around the neck and handed it back to Hussey, saying, 'We mustn't discard vital equipment.' He often talks about music being *mental medicine*. They will need more medicine than ever.

The scientists feel aggrieved. Their equipment may not be vital for survival but much of it is incredibly expensive, and on loan from learned institutions. There will be a good deal of explaining to do. *I'm sorry, the university's equipment was abandoned on an ice floe in Antarctica* – an outlandish tale if ever there was one. The scientists hope they get to tell it. There is little sympathy from the Boss for their losses and none of the scientists would go looking for it at this time. They all have a sneaking suspicion that Shackleton views science as a way of lending respectability to the expedition and acquiring sponsorship. Science was never going to help him cross the continent.

After a functional breakfast, work starts in earnest. Most men continue unloading the hold. Not everything is accessible. It's astonishing how quickly the *Endurance* has folded in on itself.

During the night blocks of ice have been forced through the hull and a good number of crates in the hold are water-logged. Supplies that are not adequately sealed will probably be tainted beyond use. Hurley's heart sinks when he sees the level of the water. His precious film and negatives will be ruined.

Saturday will be their day of departure. That gives them three days to get organised. Worsley oversees the packing of supplies on the sledges and Chippy finishes the modi-fications to the two lifeboats with timber he's pulled from the ship. Once completed, the boats will be lifted onto the sledges so they can be towed across the frozen ocean. Getting to Paulet Island is their goal but how much of the journey will be covered on foot versus on open sea is anyone's guess.

Shackleton has taken Wild with him to figure out a route to the north-west. While there are some flatter sections, most of the way forward will involve scrambling over a horribly broken-up surface and hummocky ice. Some of the more challenging obstacles, like the walls that thrust up from the surface when two ice floes collide, will need to be demolished before they can get sledges through. Both men have a growing sense of apprehension. The ice is on the move too, changing day to day. Clearing a way as they go will hopefully keep them one step ahead of the chaos.

'We'll need to organise the men into working parties,' says the Boss. 'Pathfinders, and a demolition crew with tools to attack the larger obstacles.'

'We'll need a crew to fill in the cracks too so the sledges don't tip over.'

It's another example of man versus nature. So far nature is winning. Bedevilled by the landscape, the men will retaliate with saws and hammers and shovels. Hands and feet if they need to. But the ice underfoot is far from stable.

'We mustn't let the convoy spread out over too wide an area. We must ensure everyone stays together as much as possible. I don't want anyone left behind or getting lost or separated.'

It is bound to take them a lot longer to get to open water than they had planned. Unlike their last Antarctic expedition, this is no race for a world record. This is survival, and safety is more important than speed.

CHAPTER NINE

OCTOBER–NOVEMBER 1915

Theirs is a miserable cavalcade fuelled by frustration and resentment. After four days, they have covered just over 2 kilometres. Seven dog teams have shifted more than 2000 kilograms of supplies, but the men are also harnessed to the sledges and made to pull like animals.

Every day brings fresh unpleasantness. Thick mists engulf them, heavy snow falls on them, temperatures rise and fall, everything becomes horribly wet then freezes solid. It's not just the weather that torments them; the surface itself seems intent on waylaying their progress. Hauling sledges through claggy snow leaves the men red-faced, sweaty and irritable. The surface is so deep in places that they sink to the waist. Sometimes the sun disappears and robs their surroundings of all definition. Other times the glare is so intense, the details of the landscape seem to vibrate.

By far the hardest task is hauling the lifeboats. It takes two dog teams to pull the smaller one; the larger one needs eighteen men as well as the dogs to heave it into motion. The men strain against their harnesses with gritted teeth while Captain Worsley bellows commands to keep them at their hateful task. Every now and then somebody's leg plunges through a rotten patch of ice and the unlucky man sinks to the hip. The only thing worse than the unpleasant squelch of frigid sea water in boots is the chilling thought that a fathomless ocean lies barely two feet below the surface.

'I need water,' somebody shouts from the harness.

'I've never been so thirsty,' says another man, stuffing snow into his mouth even though he knows it will make his thirst worse.

Reduced to half-rations, the men are starving, and after days of such intense physical effort, they are approaching breaking point. So too are the sledges. They were never designed to carry such heavy loads over such uneven terrain. And as for the precious lifeboats, they've been bashed and scraped and scratched, although thankfully not yet dented.

'Water,' somebody calls with real desperation. 'I can't go on without water.'

'This is complete and utter madness,' Chippy fumes.

Nobody disagrees.

They halt for the night. While the men set up the tents, Green sets about preparing the evening meal. All this loading and unloading of his cooking equipment, assembling and disassembling of the stove; he feels forever on the move, even when they rest. His back is killing him. Blackborow is sent out to look for clean snow to melt – nothing that has been churned up by feet or sledges, or is yellow or littered with dog excrement, will do for drinking water. Green opens ten cans of Irish stew to give the men a change, but he'll mix it with some pemmican to make it go further. Bits of the ship make good firewood. At least it is easy to get the fire blazing in the stove. The men are ravenous. Already a group clusters about the cook, asking how long until they eat. The chill is settling in their bones now that they have stopped moving and the wind has picked up. A few prefer to wait for supper in their sleeping bags in the relative warmth of the tents. Others have spoons at the ready and huddle close to the stove. Perhaps a little too close. Nobody sees what happens next but they all hear the cook. The stove has disintegrated, and surrendered the Irish stew to the fiery cinders – enough to feed the entire party. Green howls in anguish. Supper is ruined.

'Tea and biscuits it shall have to be,' says Blackborow.

Green just nods as he stares with incredulity at the men on their hands and knees digging into the steaming mess of food and firewood and ashes spreading slowly on the snow. Others run over and with bare hands scoop whatever they can recover of the stew into their hungry mouths, just like animals.

The Boss faces a dilemma. It was hoped that they could cover 10 kilometres a day. The sledging rations will maintain the group for only seventy days. But progress has been almost non-existent. Even on half rations, they'll run out of food. If they stay put, establish a more permanent camp on one of the sturdier floes, they can hunt down some seals and penguins to supplement their stores. They can survive at least.

Gathering Wild and Worsley in his tent, Shackleton discusses their options. By far the least appealing is to spend another winter on the ice. The best they can do is make a dash to the nearest land, but for this they'll need to launch the boats. The further north they drift, the more likely it is that the pack will open sufficiently for them to do so.

'It's going to take real patience to get through this,' says Worsley.

Shackleton is desperate for forward movement and progress. After all, he has told the men that they are going home. Once settled on a course of action, he is impatient to follow through, but he's no fool. This slow torture will destroy them. They must adapt the plan. If he has learnt one thing from all his accumulating disappointments, it's that one must always be ready to accept changing circumstances.

Relief ripples through the group when the Boss delivers his verdict. Nobody can see the sense in prolonging the agony of the march. To be comfortable and well-fed on the other hand – who could possibly argue with that? The mood is jubilant. 'Ocean Camp' is the name given to their new home on 1 November. To be close enough to their old camp that they can continue the salvaging effort is a real advantage. For one, it means going back to full rations. The thought of more food sends their spirits soaring. Little else occupies their minds. Several of the men start talking about retrieving all the bits and pieces that had to be abandoned by the ship. For all their excitement, their Dump Camp might as well be Aladdin's Cave.

CHAPTER TEN

NOVEMBER 1915

A dismal scene greets the men when they return to Dump Camp the following afternoon. The *Endurance* has slumped even lower in the ice, while the jumble of personal effects has sagged under its own weight and now sits a foot or more below the surface of the floe. They have only been gone a matter of days, but everything appears somehow distorted and foreign, partially digested by the environment.

The heavy wet snow that fell over the course of several days has solidified into an icy carapace. They will need tools to break through it. A few eager souls start to hack away at the dark tangle of clothing. It's a battle to dislodge or rip free any individual article but they work away at it with great concentration. One man strips the lid off a leather suitcase. Perfect material for repairing his boots. Another claims some woollen trousers that will be lovely and warm once he defrosts them and patches up the tear caused by yanking them out from the frozen entanglement. The frenzied rummaging continues for several hours. Those content with their accumulated loot join Chippy on the ship and help extract nails from the decking timbers.

Vincent focuses his efforts on trying to locate Hurley's hole. A few others have been strong-armed into helping with the task of digging into the rock-hard ice. Laying his hands on the buried treasures, the gold sovereigns the Boss threw in, little silver picture frames, the odd bit of jewellery. *Those fools*, he thinks. He doesn't mind carrying it. He'll carry it all the way back to England if he must. But he's had no luck so far. One item Vincent doesn't care for is Queen Alexandra's Bible. Not that he will find it in Hurley's hole. Superstitious McLeod snatched it up the second Shackleton turned his back.

'Can't have him throwing away the Good Book,' he said, sucking in his stomach and slipping the Bible into the waistband of his trousers. 'Sacrilege! We'll all be cursed like Franklin's men if we show such disregard for God's word.' The Bible is now suffering the sacrilege of smelly feet at the bottom of McLeod's sleeping bag. If the Boss found out, he'd be furious.

Aboard the partly sunken deck of the *Endurance*, Chippy and Frank Wild and a number of others spend hours removing ropes and overhanging spars and clearing tonnes of snow and ice in order to cut into a section of the decking just above their old living quarters, where extra supplies were stored. The upper deck is two feet under the water, but after rigging up a derrick and repeatedly driving a sharpened chisel into the timber, they have managed to smash a sizeable hole. A gush brings a couple of walnuts and an onion to the surface. Far from being disappointed, the men scoop them up excitedly, as if they were pure gold. Chippy uses a boat hook to rummage deeper within the darkness. A crate bobs to the surface and his face lights up in a rare smile. His technique proves surprisingly fruitful.

Crates of flour, sugar and biscuits are next; all of them seem to be well-sealed against the sea water. Everything that floats up is met with a resounding cheer. Greatly encouraged by this early success, the men dispense with the hook and strip to the waist. They plunge their bare arms under the icy water up to the shoulder. A crate of jellies floats up. Groans. Next, a crate of baking soda appears. More groans. It's scarcely worth hoping for cakes or other baked treats from Green's camp kitchen. The only thing baking soda could be used for are the bannocks that

Green has started to cook on an old sheet of iron. Filling but not delicious.

Hurley has also stripped to the waist. He's been warned off attempting to retrieve them, but his film and photographic plates are worth a fortune. He has a reputation to uphold. Groping around in ice water for close to an hour leaves him numb but ultimately victorious. It amuses him to think of the personal sacrifices he has made to get ahead in life. Carrying it all will be a struggle. He'll need to explain the extra weight to the Boss.

But Shackleton's no fool. He figured Hurley would go back for his films. And he knows dramatic images are a vital part of promoting the achievements of any expedition to the public. And generating funds. When he gets over his alarm at the photographer's risk-taking, Shackleton helps Hurley select 120 of the best images and together they smash over 400 glass plates.

Finally, when the scavenging parties return to Ocean Camp with their bounty, there is a collective sense of triumph. They have managed to haul up an additional 105 cases of provisions from the hulk. As official stores-keeper, Thomas Orde-Lees has been put in charge of arranging everything in the most rational way possible. It will take some doing; they have accumulated nearly 3 tonnes of food. Shackleton takes a keen interest in the stores-keeper's inventory. He needs to know exactly

The Boss makes no distinction. Everyone receives the same straightforward treatment. When personal grooming takes a slide, all men must submit to the shears, come what may.

Beset amid a frozen obstacle course. One would never guess that the *Endurance* is afloat on an ocean. Never again will she sail on open water.

Feeding time at the 'dogloos': the sledging teams are housed off the ship during the long dark Antarctic winter. Not one creature will survive the journey.

The dismal scene at Dump Camp: the tangled wreck of *Endurance* almost wholly digested by the ice.

Sir Ernest Shackleton leaves Britain determined the 'last great polar journey' will take one hundred and twenty days, or one short Antarctic summer.

Tom Crean, veteran and hero of Scott's ill-fated South Pole expedition, cradles the four pups he hopes will become valuable sledging dogs by spring.

Forging a path through the chaos of ice hummocks, furrows and ridges. 'They'll need pathfinders and a demolition crew with tools to attack the larger obstacles.'

Frank Hurley (left) and Ernest Shackleton at Patience Camp. 'When the sun shines, many of the men come to sit outside their tents on planks of wood and feel the warmth of summer on their faces.'

A doldrums-like existence: the rate of drift northward is far from satisfactory for men who wait so avidly for action, for open water and any hint of escape.

Launching the *James Caird* – a day of great promise and great anxiety for not only the six men bound for South Georgia but also for the twenty-two castaways on Elephant Island.

Dirty work: a penguin butchering operation in full swing on Elephant Island. Food becomes a constant preoccupation for the castaways.

Digging the ice cave – while not suitable as permanent lodgings, the cave is an adequate place to shelter while Mack and Mick amputate Blackborow's toes back at the hut.

Captain Worsley: the New Zealand skipper did not initially inspire confidence, but his navigational skills during the perilous voyage to South Georgia and his physical courage on the alpine crossing earned him the Boss's deepest respect and gratitude.

Stowaway Perce Blackborow and Mrs Chippy – firm friends from the start. The carpenter's cat would be one of the expedition's early casualties.

The Elephant Islanders – filthy, hungry and awaiting rescue, posed
in front of the cramped shelter in which they lived for five months.

One of Frank Hurley's most iconic photos. Shackleton would make
four separate attempts to rescue his men from Elephant Island.

what they have so that he can plan meals with Green and Orde-Lees. It would be good if they could eke out a normal-seeming existence over six months, but they might be on the floe for a lot longer. Each man has an aluminium mug, a spoon and a knife, but nobody thought to scavenge crockery. This has been improvised from empty tins or pieces of plywood. The spirit of invention is alive and well. Shackleton and Orde-Lees weigh the provisions using makeshift scales that Hurley has cobbled together from string and a length of wood with a provision case for a counterweight. It may not be a terribly accurate method, but approximate values are jotted down in a booklet. Like a lot of things in their new camp, it will just have to do.

'Dog pemmican,' says Orde-Lees, examining the side of the packing case. 'I'll put that aside for the dog handlers.'

'No you won't,' says Shackleton. 'We'll add that to our pantry.'

Orde-Lees looks askance. 'It's dog food.'

'This is no time to be fussy. Humans can eat dog food, if need be.'

Orde-Lees gives a shudder. 'Let's hope we don't reach that stage.'

'Amundsen went one stage further – he and his men ate their dogs.'

'Barbarism.'

'You've obviously never known starvation.'

'I have!' Orde-Lees protests. 'I felt quite light-headed on the march. Nobody had had enough to eat and even less to drink.'

Shackleton raises his eyebrows. 'I suggest you ask Wild about his experiences one day.'

'Well, judging by all this abundance,' says Orde-Lees sanctimoniously, 'we are in no danger of starving for a very long time.'

Shackleton hopes their ice floe home will last months rather than weeks. There's far too much to carry with them if they should need to set off in a hurry to find a new campsite, or if the pack ice broke up suddenly and they needed to launch the lifeboats. It would be a tragedy to abandon tonnes of good food. They would be forced to gorge themselves silly, only to face starvation weeks later.

Orde-Lees makes a mental note to add eating dog food to his growing list of unpleasant things he may have to get used to. Not being able to wash is loathsome. There is no water for washing. Pots and bodies are scoured with snow without the benefit of soap. He finds the filthy state of his hands distressing. At least the muck on his palms rubs off on the inside of his gloves. And going to the toilet is humiliating. He finds the latrines appalling. Down go the trousers. Out in the open a man must be quick to the business. Human waste is often gobbled up by dogs. Even fought over.

Oh, what a scene of squalor and degradation, thinks Orde-Lees.

The sleeping arrangements leave a lot to be desired too. He would gladly put up with Jimmy's messy habits if it meant being back in their cabin on the ship. In the big tent at night the men are so confined that they press together like sardines in a tin. Nobody can move. Nobody can leave the tent without inadvertently standing on someone's arm or leg and provoking an outburst or a thump. Warmth is one benefit to be enjoyed, bodily odours are not.

There have been threats made against Orde-Lees. His snoring is the source of all the bother. His tent mates have warned him that they're close to throwing him out. Perhaps it would be a good thing. He could sleep on his own amid the provision crates. He could keep an eye on things. It's only a matter of time before one of the sailors tries to pinch some extra food. Having seen how Vincent dug around so intently in the jumble of personal belongings back at Dump Camp, Orde-Lees is not sure he would trust the man to look after his morning toast – he'd have the crusts off and the centre hollowed out before you could say 'knife'.

The flurry of activity at Ocean Camp has done nothing to scare off the wildlife. Curious enough to investigate at close range, all the local visitors meet the same sad fate as Mrs Chippy and Crean's puppies – although they don't end up in a hole. Both as a source of food and of fuel, seals and penguins are becoming an even more precious commodity than before. So much so that generally there is somebody keeping an eye out for any game from the elevated lookout platform that the men have erected using pieces of planking from the wreck. There's something of a child's fort about it, with its mast flying the Union Jack and a pennant from the Royal Clyde Yacht Club flapping cheerfully in breeze. Every now and then there are excited shouts from whoever is on lookout duty and the hunt is on. Officially speaking, it's vital to their survival, but in the middle of the Weddell Sea, it's the closest any of them get to actually having fun.

The early days of Ocean Camp are long. Most men drop off to sleep after supper without any trouble. Night watch will keep some up beyond bedtime. Each watch is an hour and involves walking the perimeter of the camp, registering any irregularities in the surface, and keeping an eye on trouble spots. Every now and then cracks appear and the floes separate, revealing a dark sweep of ocean. Sometimes orcas come up to blow fountains of foul-smelling mist high into the air. The spurting sound that accompanies this impressive display often catches the men off guard, especially if they're standing close to the edge. They tend to stare longingly at any glimpse of ocean. Nothing stays open for long, however. The water either freezes over again or pressure brings the floes back together. Any hint of impending freedom is fleeting.

The Boss is always the last man to turn in and generally engages whoever is on night watch in conversation. A deep tiredness overwhelms him in the evenings, but it doesn't concentrate its weight in his arms and legs. Instead it stretches across his brow and down the sides of his face. He is exhausted by smiles. His throat aches with the jokes and the banter that have buoyed his men throughout another day. Sometimes it's an act. Sometimes all he feels is a gnawing sense of doubt. Despite the general excitement of establishing Ocean Camp, the Boss is acutely aware that they cannot become complacent. Their floe is a thick one, older, more substantial and flatter than those in the immediate vicinity, but it could buckle or concertina or erupt violently at any time, just like the floes around them.

In the morning he'll discuss emergency plans with Wild. Each man should be assigned a specific task. Should a move become necessary, they'll need to act with maximum efficiency. Situations deteriorate quickly on the ice. Crean can be put in charge of preparing the sledges; he'll do a good job of packing them with essentials. In the event of catastrophe, hauling these sledges to safety will take precedence over any other task. How fortunate to have old friends, trusted companions. It's a relief to be able to delegate to such men. If only he could hand it all over.

'Old Shack'

Seven Seas, 1890

From one hemisphere to the next, from schoolboy to sailor. The transition has not been easy. The sixteen-year-old finds himself shaved, tarred and dunked in a bucket of sea water by King Neptune. Thankfully, Ernest is over his crippling seasickness by the time he must endure the Crossing of the Line initiation.

Never has he spent more than a week away from his family and yet it is not homesickness but exhilaration that accompanies him on his maiden voyage from Liverpool to Valparaiso aboard the Hoghton Tower. *A whole year at sea. In the dim and unseemly crew's quarters he clutches his Bible to his chest and says his prayers,* surrounded by grubby men whose foul language and drunkenness is like nothing he's ever witnessed before.

Captain Partridge is wise and generous and answers Ernest's questions in an unhurried way. The crew show similar patience with the lad so unschooled in the basic principles of sailing, and ignorant of the wide seas and the southern gales that snap spars and dash out brains.

Ernest performs well under pressure, remains unruffled by the heavy weather off Cape Horn that is as severe as anything the seasoned shellbacks have lived through. Sent aloft in the storm, Ernest howls with terror and delight into the prevailing winds, safe in the knowledge that nobody can hear him over the sound of waves crashing over the bow 45 metres below. But they see his face and recognise his glee. It's exactly what brings them back to the seafaring life again and again.

After the storm the men take to calling him 'Old Shack'. Even though he's the youngest, he's the one who sings with the loudest voice while pulling on the ropes. They like that about him, and the fact that he takes anything in his stride, laughs with the fiercest and shows his mettle below deck. They share their tobacco. They like his poetry too. His Bible less so.

'He's the most pig-headed, obstinate boy I have ever come across,' says Captain Partridge when they complete their voyage of 40,000 kilometres. 'And I'll take him back any time.'

Back home with family, Old Shack welcomes his sisters' kisses but the walls of the house oppress him. He longs to continue his *open-air geography lessons in the company of men who can spin a yarn and reef a sail.*

When once again he puts to sea aboard the Hoghton Tower, *shipping rice and hay and nitrates from Iquique to India, Ernest finds himself writing letter after letter to his sisters. Through cresting waves he devotes himself to perfecting the art of seamanship. He cheats death and learns to swear and quotes Swinburne's poetry to his crewmates, but homesickness finds him sure enough, and no amount of time aloft can sweep its blackness from his heart.* What can have changed? *he wonders. The ship is the same, the men just as hearty as they were the first time he set sail. Exotic ports and wild steely seas bring great excitement, but at the helm is a very different captain. A harsh disciplinarian and utterly indifferent to his men, Captain Robinson is the complete opposite of Captain Partridge. He may be their leader, but it is only in name.*

CHAPTER ELEVEN

NOVEMBER 1915

It's late afternoon on 21 November and the Boss is shouting from the lookout platform. Men scramble from their tents to witness what has been anticipated for weeks. The November sky is streaked with colour, a vast backdrop for the drama unfolding before their eyes. So long locked in place, cradled by the ice, the *Endurance* is suddenly a dark thing shivering into position. From several kilometres away they watch her death throes back at Dump Camp. The whole thing barely lasts ten minutes. Slowly her bow begins the downward slide, while her stern rises elegantly like a ballerina on pointe.

It's a violent end. Buckling metal, cracking timbers. The sound of her hull finally collapsing must surely be deafening. By the time it reaches their ears, it's barely a whisper.

'She's gone, boys,' says Shackleton.

They stand about like statues. Blackborow lets out a groan of disbelief. The sentiment is echoed throughout the group in a series of wordless utterances. Shackleton puts a comforting arm around the former stowaway. The Boss has neither words nor poetry. Blackborow smears away tears. Of course, the ship was useless. Without her masts, the hull punctured beyond repair, it was hardly a source of hope. But she was a symbolic link with the outside world. And now she is gone.

'So that's that,' says Shackleton plainly.

The men look at each other with a mixture of resignation and regret. What happens now?

'I'm not a landlubber. I don't belong on land,' says Vincent, as though his refusal to accept their fate is all that's required to change it.

'You're not really on land, are you?' someone suggests.

'Doesn't make much difference.' Captain Worsley's words are almost too quiet to hear. Suddenly he is a captain without a ship – that's reason enough to cry. And to think a year or more ago, he was conveying his prophetic dream of ice and adventure to Frank Wild in the expedition offices on New Burlington Street in London. He certainly didn't prophesy this. How swiftly dreams turn to nightmares in this godforsaken place.

'I know how you feel, mate,' Hurley says to the captain with his characteristic brashness.

Worsley looks doubtful as he wipes away his tears.

'My work's gone down the gurgler too. I'm a bloody photographer and I've got three measly rolls of unprocessed film to my name. How do you think that makes me feel?'

Neither man sees the point in standing around watching the hole in the pack ice slowly freeze over. The two men fall into step.

'I'm not sorry to see the last of that wreck,' says Hurley. 'Bloody depressing sight if you ask me.'

Worsley is used to Hurley's flippant comments. Some find his abrasive manner irritating. Worsley is just pleased for the distraction. He'd like to banish the alarming image of the *Endurance* sinking from his mind. He allows the photographer to lead him away to where the largest of the three lifeboats sits on a sledge.

'Now here's a fine vessel for you, Skip. Not too big. Solid as a rock. See how the carpenter has raised the bulwarks? Look, they're a whole foot higher. He needs to finish decking her over, then she'll be good to go. And the other two lifeboats – it won't take us long to make them seaworthy. I've even made a pump so we won't have to bail like mad with a teacup and a rusty tablespoon.'

Worsley nods at Hurley's attempt at light-heartedness. 'Thank goodness the Boss finally agreed to bring the third lifeboat up from the wreck. I was losing sleep over who we would have to leave behind.'

'Ahh, what about the poor dogs?' says Hurley.

'The price of adventure,' says Worsley.

'Speaking of adventure,' Hurley says, 'did I ever tell you that my mum wrote to Douglas Mawson and told him not to take me to Antarctica? She said my health was poor. Said the trip would kill me.'

'Mawson ignored her advice – lucky for you,' Worsley grins.

'And then, you know what? Mawson warned me not to come to Antarctica with Shackleton.' Hurley roars with laughter. 'Wish I hadn't ignored his advice!'

Hearing laughter, several others gather to the lifeboats. Doctors Macklin and McIlroy, Wild and Blackborow and Green, Jimmy and Orde-Lees, the scientists Clark and Wordie. Everyone wants to touch the lifeboats, run their hands over the bulwarks or slap the side of the hull like they were lucky charms. One of these days the ice will break up properly and they will actually launch them.

On this most dismal of evenings, nobody wants to head back into the tents. They crave company and conversation, even if muted. Some of the men try to look on the bright side – they're free to move on now. Frank Wild lights his pipe and smokes in silence as though he's just lost an old friend. Others, like superstitious McLeod, can't help but see everything in the blackest terms.

'Where's the Boss?' someone asks.

Jimmy says, 'He went back to his tent.'

'He's usually got some fighting words,' says Dr Macklin.

'It's a savage blow,' says Wild. 'He just needs . . .'

Hurley interrupts. 'What happened to your glasses, Jimmy?'

Jimmy blinks behind cracked lenses. 'Bit of bad luck, I dare say.'

Wild says, 'Bit more than bad luck. Blimey.'

Jimmy offers a nervous smile. 'Can't be helped. They slipped off my head and somebody trod on them before I could pick them up.'

'Can you still read?' Hurley's first thought is for the encyclopaedias.

'I'll manage,' Jimmy says, blinking.

'You'll have to grab a rifle and join the hunting party,' says Dr Macklin, patting him on the back. His comment raises a laugh. The thought of the clumsiest man on the ice wielding a firearm is preposterous.

'I don't think I should, actually,' says Jimmy earnestly. 'Without my glasses, I won't be a very good shot.'

'Perhaps for once he can help butcher the carcasses.' Vincent's comment is a snide one, not as well-intentioned as

Dr Macklin's. He's fishing for a laugh too. Everyone knows Jimmy has been 'let off' all but the most basic chores.

'So who was the silly bastard who stomped on your glasses?' Hurley probes.

Jimmy looks straight ahead as though he hasn't heard the question and pushes his bent frames back up his nose.

Vincent is quick to change the subject. 'We're true castaways – that is what we have become, lads.'

Without a doubt, they are the most isolated humans on the planet. Unreachable, perhaps even forgotten.

Shackleton wakes early after a fitful night's rest. Thoughts flood in as he listens to the rustle of the canvas in the wind and the muffled sounds of slumbering men around him. He sags at the impossible task before him. How to bridge the yawning gap between how he feels and how he must appear when he steps from this tent? He unfolds the Kipling from his pocket and reads it, enjoying the familiar rhythm of the words.

> *And so hold on when there is nothing in you*
> *Except the Will which says to them: 'Hold on!'*

Enough for now. Nobody wants to hear about his frail health, his doubts or his desire to withdraw into himself – they want a leader. An inspiring one. A Captain Partridge rather than a Captain Robinson. And so he must lead.

Oily fumes are already billowing from the blubber stove when the Boss appears. Blackborow is busy mixing up the fat and flour to form the morning's bannocks but Green is wittering in a high-pitched way that can only mean one thing.

'The Belly Burglar's been at it again,' he says, showing the Boss the meagre rations doled out by the stores-keeper.

This is definitely not the morning for Orde-Lees to demonstrate his natural tendency for frugality.

'Orde-Lees!' calls the Boss with obvious irritation. 'What do you call this?'

'One and a half sausages per man is quite sufficient,' he says.

'But they're tiny sausages!'

Orde-Lees closes his eyes in a self-righteous way. 'You gave me authority over our stores . . .'

'And I have authority over you!' interrupts Shackleton. 'The men need food! You will provide it. That is an order.'

Orde-Lees screws up his mouth with displeasure. 'Sausages are a luxury. A moderate helping should be enough.' He slowly crosses his arms across his chest in a gesture that anyone else would find intimidating. He's a big man.

But his posturing has no effect on the Boss. 'Two. Sausages. Per. Man,' he says, emphasising each word, before leaving.

Orde-Lees shouts after him: 'We really should be stock-piling seal meat – we're going to need it in the long run!'

Shackleton doesn't respond. Stockpiling seal meat? That's the last thing he wants to do. The moment that happens, he'll lose men. Simple men like Vincent and McLeod, argumentative Hubert Hudson, untested types like Jimmy and Blackborow, even older hands like Chippy. *As soon as there's mention of stockpiling seals and penguins, they'll think we're stuck here forever.* The fragile order he has established will evaporate into thin air. No man must be allowed to fall into despair. No man must think that their situation is anything other than a temporary inconvenience.

CHAPTER TWELVE

NOVEMBER–DECEMBER 1915

There are no outward signs that they are drifting north. A slow parade of icebergs is the only indication that their world is in motion. If anyone should doubt that they are making headway, the captain has irrefutable proof. Worsley may no longer have a ship, but he continues to maintain a log like a good skipper. Every day he records their latitude and longitude and ascertains the rate and direction of their drift.

Pleasing progress can be reported to the Boss. In the five weeks since they abandoned the ship, they have been carried 190 kilometres. All of it in the right direction. If only

Worsley could command the floe as he would a vessel. He could set a course, instruct the men to make ready the sails. Sadly, he is helpless in this regard. The floe does not respond to his insults or fervent prayers but only to the commands issued by fickle winds.

A watched pot never boils – Worsley often thinks of this old saying and wonders if they would go faster if he was not counting every kilometre and noting it so diligently in his logbook. When it comes to speed, warm days are worst; they make virtually no headway at all. A bitter southerly, on the other hand, sets them in the right direction and is worth the red sting of frozen faces. A blizzard is even better, a true blessing. Confined to their tents on such days, it may feel like the hours drag, but Ocean Camp is blown terrific distances. The record so far is almost 40 kilometres over a three-day period.

Sometimes Blackborow assists the captain. His education need not be abandoned simply because their ship lies on the seabed. The way Worsley sees it, the lad might as well learn the basics of navigation as mix up bannocks for the griddle. When the sun or stars are visible, Worsley shows him how to take readings with the theodolite to establish their latitude. Marine chronometers and navigation tables take care of the longitude.

'The chronometers must be wound every day and at the same time,' Worsley says. 'It is absolutely critical. Otherwise they'll lose accuracy. They won't be any use at all. We won't have a bloody clue where we are.'

On dull days when the sun disappears, dead reckoning is all Worsley can fall back on, but he's an expert at that. It's always a joy when he takes an actual reading and finds his estimates are bang on. Blackborow is impressed. So are all the sailors. Shackleton realises he was wrong about Worsley, misjudged him from the start of the voyage. Far from being flighty and untrustworthy, he's an absolute asset.

Like Hurley, the captain has a knack for invention. Worsley is especially proud of his latest innovation – a contraption he's rigged up to determine what's happening under the floe. A rod fitted with a vane is inserted into a metal tube that has been frozen into the pack. Acting like an underwater weathervane, Worsley's creation indicates the direction of their drift. The scientists have all complimented him on his ingenuity. Its simplicity mocks the sophisticated scientific instrumentation that lies abandoned and accumulating layers of rime at Dump Camp. For all the good this equipment has done mankind on this expedition, it might as well serve as firewood.

Any activity that breaks the boredom is seized on by all. While out hunting for seals, Dr Macklin and Wordie paddle a small raft of sea ice across a widening lead of water. They holler like schoolboys punting on the river. Others gather on the edge to watch the spectacle. There's some discussion about whether they should organise some races on the black water to raise spirits.

Crean shakes his head in bewilderment. 'Get back in here, Mack!'

Orcas are becoming an increasingly common sight around the edges of the loosening pack. He tosses them a rope to fetch them from danger. It wouldn't take much of a nudge to unseat these two fools. On Scott's *Terra Nova* expedition, he's seen killer whales burst through half a metre of solid sea ice to snatch at a man. And he'll never forget the ghastly sight of a pony flailing in the water amid a whole pod of the evil creatures. Not surprisingly, Shackleton is furious when he finds out. The men have started to call him 'Cautious Jack'.

Hurley helps haul them to safety, feeling a bit guilty as he remembers his own recent brush with death while exercising one of the dog teams. A moment's inattention, a sinking sledge, dogs paddling like mad, his heart bursting through his chest, one phrase racing through his mind: *this is how it all ends*. He didn't tell the Boss. He doesn't need a telling-off. He knows perfectly well that it was an idiotic idea to take a nap on the sledge in the sun.

November passes into December. These are bad days, with the temperature hovering just above freezing, when pools of water form on the surface. Sinkholes form under damp sleeping bags. The tents start to smell of rotting hide. During certain windless periods when the sun beats down on the canvas, the interior of the tents reaches the high twenties and the men throw open the doors and hoist the back wall to let the air flow through. At night the mercury drops. Breath gathers in fine ice crystals above their heads only to rain down again like a fine indoor snow in the morning.

McLeod winces as he settles his body into clammy fur, no longer sure if it is such a blessing to be the proud owner of one of the reindeer sleeping bags. He pulls the Bible out and flicks open its damp pages, which are covered in coarse hairs. He shakes his hand vigorously, but they stick to his skin. They cling to everything in the tent. Faces, clothing, cutlery. The men have grown accustomed to finding reindeer fur in virtually every mouthful. Sometimes they swear, full of rage, at the futility of shaking out their bedding and cleaning out the tent. Why bother?

Then again, why bother doing anything? The mood is the same in all the tents. So much of each day is spent lying around in the never-ending daylight, with no desire to do anything other than observe the subtle motions of the fabric overhead. Even as summer approaches, subtle signs of depression appear like small bubbles in a soon-to-be-boiling pot of water. They don't discuss the war anymore. They don't mention their families or the fact that Christmas is fast approaching and they are no closer to getting home.

The slow decay of the ice seems to be the only topic of conversation. The edges of their floating home are crumbling. Their floe is getting smaller. It's time to get moving again.

The Boss has an announcement. Christmas will be celebrated several days early this year so they can pack up and resume their march over the floes. The direction of drift is off. They're tracking too far east for Paulet Island. Westward is the direction to go. Despite launching one of the boats in a nearby lead, nobody expects they'll be able to take to the water yet. It's just a test, but even after the complication of hauling it back onto the ice, the men take it as an encouraging sign. It feels good to have a purpose, a group activity that breaks the monotony of camp life even if the promise of escape cannot be fulfilled just yet. There's no rhyme or reason to the way the floes behave. Nobody can predict how or when they'll drift apart sufficiently to launch all three boats. For the moment there is no network of leads they can navigate to the open water. At the same time, if they remain at Ocean Camp, they'll end up sinking or living on a floe the size of a postage stamp.

Shackleton and Crean, Hurley and Wild set out with dog teams to survey a potential route. The surface is blighted with soft snow, but the pressure ridges don't pose as much of a problem as last time. Again, they'll jettison all non-essential items and try to make the sledges as light as possible.

'We're guaranteed a white Christmas at least,' says Blackborow as he helps the captain pack away his navigation tables.

'Yes indeed,' Worsley sighs. 'But you'll hear curses not carols ringing out.'

When the sun shines and the wind drops, many of the men come to sit outside their tents on planks of wood or empty crates and feel the warmth of summer on their faces.

Conversations weave as they mend socks or read books or simply enjoy their dwindling reserves of tobacco. For a short time it's possible to imagine they are living a life elsewhere. They could be at a pub, or dangling their feet off a wharf, shooting the breeze during a tea break. For a short time they can forget that they will soon be on the dreaded march.

'We won't be needing this.' Vincent touches a match to the twist of fine paper and lights his pipe. 'Not a bad use for an encyclopaedia,' he grins.

'You're a philistine,' harrumphs Chippy.

'I've no idea what you're talking about, old man,' says Vincent, blowing smoke rings.

'Look it up under "P", there might be a picture of you,' Chippy mutters, and returns pointedly to his book.

Vincent is restless. If he were a dog, he'd be starting to chew shoes; instead he's acting in a deliberately provocative way. Not that tearing pages from the *Encyclopaedia Britannica* and setting fire to them is going to rile many. The ones like Jimmy who have been consuming the volumes have already torn out the pages they want to keep. Chippy has his own reading material – McClintock's quest to find Franklin's lost expedition. Every now and then he gives a grunt. 'Curse them,' he spits.

'Curse who?'

'The British government.'

'What have they got to do with anything?'

'Made Lady Franklin organise everything. Her husband lost in the Arctic, locked in the ice most probably. And they won't lift a finger to go look for them.'

'Who cares?' says Vincent.

'You'd do well to read this book,' says Chippy. 'Their situation was not so different from your own.'

Green asks, 'Remind me, Chippy, what happened to them?'

'Not sure I should tell a cook.'

'Go on,' says Vincent.

Chippy wets his lips and says, 'Well, they ran out of food and then they ate each other.'

Vincent laughs. 'Lousy stew you'd make, old man.'

'If that was us, who do you reckon we would we eat first?' someone asks.

'Orde-Lees!'

'He's a big man. There's a lot of meat on him.'

Green cackles. 'And with the Belly Burgler out of the picture, we'd finally get our hands on some proper rations.'

CHAPTER THIRTEEN

DECEMBER 1915

A disgruntled man is a dangerous one, and Chippy is far from happy. Three days on the move, three days of hard slog, three days of gasping for breath. Hauling the lifeboats proves just as hard as it was on their first attempt to cross the floes. Once before they abandoned the march; it seems inevitable that their current labours will end in similar frustration.

With his face set in a sour expression, Chippy thinks about John Franklin's men towing their boats across an icy wasteland to their deaths. He calculates their own chances of survival as slim. Chippy has a pinched nerve from straining against his harness and his piles are throbbing like never before.

Every day he watches with growing scepticism as Wild and Shackleton set out from the tents to reconnoitre the day's route. Their optimistic appraisals make him angry. Five kilometres the Boss says they will need to cover and yet the men barely manage to move the boats 50 metres before collapsing to their knees. And the back and forth of relaying means doubling the effort. It would be a lucky day if they managed to travel one kilometre. How the Boss imagines they can make meaningful headway towards Paulet Island, he cannot say. Even if they could pick up the pace, to match the Boss's overly ambitious target, it would take six months to reach their goal. Much easier to be a dog, oblivious to everything, than be a man who can see the whole disaster unfolding.

Chippy knows that they are carrying barely forty days of food. Why doesn't anyone say anything? Even Orde-Lees and the cook trudge on, their sledge piled high with cooking equipment, apparently happy to be on the move. Of all people, they should have realised that starvation is in store. The thought bears down on him. They are doomed to fail just like Franklin. Why will nobody acknowledge this simple fact? Instead it is the sheer weight of the boats that is the focus of the men's grousing. And in his current pessimistic state, Chippy cannot help but take all the criticism personally.

'Why'd you make these lifeboats so bloody heavy, Chippy?'

'I had to build up the bulwarks to keep out the water,' the carpenter says defensively. 'She's a whole foot higher. She had to be. Then all the added weight from decking her over halfway too. Course she's heavy to pull. A boat is not designed to pull. A boat needs to float.'

'I doubt there'll be enough room for us all,' one of the scientists says.

Chippy is quiet for a time. His lips move back and forth over his teeth as if he is trying to dislodge a thought that has taken hold in his mind. 'I told the Boss I could build a sloop from salvage timbers. It would have been big enough for everybody to fit in.'

'This is hard enough. Pulling a sloop would be impossible!'

'I was never suggesting that!' Chippy shouts. 'Why pull anything? The drift is carrying us northward! But no, the Boss didn't want to know about my sloop idea – he has his own ideas about getting us on the move. And here we are, dragging loads like . . .' The carpenter's words trail off. He wants to say '. . . *dragging loads like Franklin's men.*' But he won't say any more. There's no point. Why describe how, after dragging their boats across polar wastes, Franklin's men turned to cannibalism.

*

Travel at night offers the advantage of slightly cooler temperatures, and therefore a firmer surface underfoot. It doesn't feel like night – it never gets dark now. The sun sits low in the sky, ever watchful. Only briefly does it blink, touching the horizon around midnight before it returns its wary eye to the raggle-taggle procession inching north-west across the seemingly endless ice floes.

When they turn in after a day's march, it's warmer in the tents – some say too hot. The men drift into the dreamless sleep of the exhausted. Some prefer to doss down on the snow in the fresh air under the blaze of midday sun, shielding their faces under blankets or excess clothing.

After consuming a breakfast of cold mutton and tea at 5pm, the men break into their work groups – the trail breakers head away with their tools to clear a path for the dog handlers to smooth down with their teams and make ready for the boat haulers, those unfortunates who yoke up like beasts to tackle the impossible. Captain Worsley encourages them as best he can, but his veneer of enthusiasm is wearing thin. Doubts about their plan are hard to shake. His binoculars return repeatedly to the third lifeboat they left behind at Ocean Camp. The Boss insisted he leave a note tucked into a gunwale. The message *All Well* now seems completely inappropriate. Things are far from well. Worsley agrees wholeheartedly that being on the move is better than sitting around, but he finds it increasingly hard to maintain the level of optimism shown by the Boss.

Shackleton has been talking loudly about grand plans for his next expedition. It will be to Alaska. Never one to shy away from adventure, Worsley was an excited participant in such discussions. For a time, it was an amusing pastime. But in recent days he finds himself exhausted by the very idea of further schemes. The next twelve hours is the only future he can envisage. Life is a struggle with an increasingly fractious crew that will not be able to handle much more of this dreadful pulling.

The march is not just hard work; it's becoming more dangerous. Thin ice, broken ice – both claim men. Tom Crean slides through a crack and into water. His arms thrash about as he struggles to gain purchase on the slippery edge. Crean tries to grasp at all the hands reaching for him, but his wet clothing and boots drag him lower. His head goes under. The cold hits him between the eyes with pure white pain that invades his entire body. Grabbing handfuls of waterlogged clothing, a group of men somehow haul him to the surface. He cannot speak. A grimace is all he manages before the shaking kicks in. Uncontrollable spasms ripple through his core and down his legs while his hands stiffen to claws. He is as helpless as a baby. It's Worsley who springs to action, stripping off the sodden garments that are already developing a fine layer of frost in the biting air.

'Clothes!' he shouts.

Nobody has anything to spare, but the sight of Crean, naked and shivering and thin as a skinned rabbit on the ice, is horrifying enough to get the men peeling back their layers. Woollens, a hat, mitts, socks are handed over. One man takes off his trousers, leaving only the meagre protection of long-johns on his own skinny limbs. Cowering in the lee of one of the lifeboats, Crean is grateful for every stitch of clothing. Despite their willingness to help, the selfless owners all watch the Irishman regain his strength with the avid hope he'll get back into his own clothes before too long.

They pass a sombre few hours after Crean's brush with death. Everything seems worse because they are colder, but they have also received a stark reminder of the danger they face. Every time they stop for a rest, sounds of despair and resentment rise above the assembled group. At the centre, the muttering is always Chippy.

'Don't you start! I worked a miracle. We're in the middle of nowhere, I've got no tools. A saw and a hammer. And an adze,' Chippy fumes. 'And as for caulking the timbers! Oakum from unravelling rope. Probably the first time ever that somebody used artist's oil paints to seal the joins.'

'Chippy,' says Worsley. 'Calm down. Nobody's disputing your skill. Come on. Get in your harness.'

The carpenter blinks at the captain and says simply, 'I won't.'

'What do you mean, you won't? Get into your harness. You're holding us up.'

'You can go on without me. I'll not move any further on this ridiculous march.'

'Captain's orders!'

'Funny sort of captain! You don't have a ship. You don't have a command. And I'll not move any further – you can order me until you're blue in the face.'

Worsley is taken aback. He has no words for Chippy, who folds his arms across his chest while the assembled crew watch with growing unease.

'Don't be a fool!' someone shouts.

'Come on, you old goat,' says Orde-Lees. 'Do as you're told.'

'Go to hell!' shouts Chippy. The dogs start to bark. The men start their own discussions.

Worsley takes Chippy roughly by the elbow and steers him off to the side. 'This won't end well for you.'

Chippy wrestles his arm free and rejoins the group, shouting, 'This won't end well for any of us!'

Confused by the delay, Shackleton and Wild return to find Worsley and Hurley in a huddle. Worsley has never been a hard taskmaster or a strict enforcer of discipline. He's known sailors to transgress from time to time, misbehave on shore, even engage in insubordinate behaviour on the ship, but nine times out of ten he would prefer to let things slide. In his experience seamen simply need an opportunity to let off steam now and then. But this is different.

'He's out of line, Skip,' Hurley says. 'You've got to come down on him like a tonne of bricks or the others might decide they're not moving either. There are a lot of worried blokes. This could flip them.'

'The trouble is, he's right,' Worsley says in a low voice. 'This *is* pointless.'

For Chippy to challenge Worsley's authority as the captain of a non-existent vessel is one thing, but loyalty is at stake here. Shackleton's ability to lead them to safety is holding the whole fragile situation together. If the men can't believe in their leader, there will be a mutiny. Worsley is relieved when the Boss steps in and takes control.

'Nonsense,' he says plainly. 'Chippy doesn't know what he's talking about.'

The Boss is not as calm as his demeanour would suggest. The situation is deeply troubling. This is the closest they have come to crisis. The carpenter couldn't have chosen a worse time. He can feel his anger rising. None of the men notice. They watch as Worsley and Wild, Shackleton and Hurley confer, wondering what will come of the carpenter's one-man rebellion. When the Boss walks off, deep in conversation with Wild, nobody knows where they're going.

Blackborow is perplexed. 'I don't understand what's happening. Why is everyone just standing around?' he asks the cook.

'Don't know,' is Green's reply. 'But that Chippy is going to find himself in hot water.'

The Ship's Articles is what the Boss wants to dig out from his personal papers – all the crew have signed up to this contract. He is keen to remind them about their responsibilities. On the face of it, this is a technical issue – something lawyers might be called on to fix; and it would be fixed swiftly under normal circumstances. But without a ship, it is a meaningless piece of paper. Disobeying orders carries serious consequences in wartime. Are they not facing a similar crisis, fighting for their lives on a disintegrating ice floe?

Shackleton's voice is tense. 'Frank. We may need to shoot him.'

Frank Wild nods. 'Well, I guess it will be me. As leader, you can't.'

'Let's hope we can resolve this another way.'

'*And the Crew agree to conduct themselves in an orderly, faithful, honest and sober manner, and to be at all times diligent in their respective Duties and to be obedient to the lawful commands of the said Master ...*' Shackleton pauses and looks directly at Chippy. '*... disobedience to lawful commands will be legally punishable ...*'

Murmurs rise from the men, a few shift their feet; there are one or two nervous coughs.

Blackborow whispers, 'What does that mean?'

'Shhh,' Green hisses.

Shackleton's voice is strong and clear. 'Ship's Articles have not terminated with the sinking of *Endurance*. It says so here.' He taps the papers for emphasis.

Wild smiles at Worsley. The captain looks confused. He knows the contract says nothing of the sort.

Shackleton continues, 'You will remain on full pay until we reach port.'

The captain suddenly understands. It's not how it works. Usually when a ship sinks, the wages cease. Shackleton is making it all up, but nothing will cause these men to question the authority of a man who assures them of full pay. If Chippy were looking for others to join his rebellion, he will be sorely disappointed. The Boss has taken the wind from his sails. And, as the Boss will soon advise him, he will need to get back into line or pay with his life.

'Three cheers for the Boss!' someone hollers.

Green leans close to Blackborow. 'If you haven't already lad, best be signing your name to that document.'

'SHACKLES'

DISCOVERY EXPEDITION, ANTARCTICA 1902

The dogs trail behind the sledge, skinny, disloyal, attacking each other while the three men forge ahead, resigned to pulling their own equipment and dwindling provisions. For more than a month they've headed south across the frozen face of the Great Ice Barrier. The dogs whimper and fall further back. Manhauling is the only way to make progress now. Determined as ever that their suffering should mean something, Captain Scott and Dr Wilson make good companions in miserable times. They call him Shackles; when they can hear each other over the howling wind, that is.

Each forced step tames new land. This is the essence of

exploring – men conquering virgin territory. To be the first to venture this far into the Antarctic interior is fine motivation for the march, even if more whiteness is the reward. They can already claim a new world record: furthest south. Of course, they want more. The South Pole is the goal. If only it did not come at a dreadful cost. Faces ravaged, half-starved, they feel as wretched as their animals.

By New Year's Eve, the dogs are dead and the men call a halt to their ambitions. It will be a desperate struggle to undertake the 480 kilometres back to their base on the frozen coast. Only their blood-shot eyes will stray beyond this point; to the mountains at 83 degrees south. Perhaps others will get further. Each man hopes to try again. Shackles certainly does, but in his current weakened state, his first objective must be to survive the journey home.

More than anything, Shackles fears the coughing fits, paralysing in intensity, arriving with a violence far beyond anything he thought his body capable of withstanding. And then there's the blood, gobs of it, splattering onto the snow by day, bursting from his mouth across the sleeping bag at night.

'He won't last,' Dr Wilson murmurs as the tent rattles in the gale.

Shackles is peeled apart by pain as the cough's fury penetrates deeper into his lungs. He feels life being ripped from him as easily as pages being torn from a book while Wilson's fearful words ring in his ears. But there are other words in his head telling him, 'Hold on!'

In the morning he effects a standing position on numb feet. It is by some miracle that he can walk. Perhaps it is to prove

Dr Wilson wrong. Perhaps to prove Antarctica wrong. Too weak to pull the sledge, Shackles seeks to distract his mind with poetry. Lines from Kipling thump in his ears – 'If you can trust yourself when all men doubt you . . .' – while his feet maintain their slow rhythm in the snow.

Scott and Wilson can barely carry their own wasted frames through swirling drift, but Shackleton can feel their eyes on him. He senses their concern at his worsening condition. His gums are swollen. His limbs ache with scurvy. To be towed by his comrades on the sledge, a dead weight, is the ultimate humiliation. Shackles is at his lowest ebb. No longer does he care about the newsmen or the record keepers. He wants to survive – if only for another chance to venture south.

When the relief ship carries him away from Antarctica, Shackles weeps with sadness and frustration. Two doctors have examined him, declared him an invalid. Suffering from exhaustion, his heart and lungs permanently damaged by the southern journey, he cannot possibly remain with Scott and Wilson for another year on the ice. As leader of the Discovery expedition, Scott has the final say and Shackles must accept his decision. They will stay and he will go.

The three parting cheers from his comrades are a moving tribute. He cares little if others see him crying. What are tears when a man is being torn from his ambitions? What feats of courage and endurance will it take to conquer the unimaginable immensity of Antarctica? He gave every ounce of strength, almost surrendered *his life to achieve something of worth, and still 1000 kilometres lay between him and greatness. Shackles dries his tears and gazes at the mountains that refuse to surrender the horizon even as the silver shoreline fades from view. So too, will he refuse to surrender, to give up on the south.* By Endurance We Conquer *is the Shackleton family motto. He will bring this virtue to bear yet, on this terrible and wondrous continent. When he returns. When he is leader of his own Antarctic expedition.*

CHAPTER FOURTEEN

DECEMBER 1915

Retreat is a poor reward for everything they have suffered. The men are on the brink of total exhaustion. The dogs are hungry and turning more savage with each passing day. For all their pain, they are only 12 kilometres from Ocean Camp. There is no hope of advancing further across the pack ice. There's nothing but slushy ice ahead – that's the conclusion Shackleton has reached after trying to scout a route with Wild. Instead they'll call a halt and wait for the leads to open up. Only the sea and the ocean currents will decide their fate.

It takes four hours to backtrack a kilometre to the previous evening's camp site. Defeated, the men turn in without saying a word. Chippy was right; he had it figured out several days ago, that they could never haul these boats the necessary distance. Frustration hangs in the air. Chippy himself doesn't think it wise to say, *I told you so*. A few men write disparaging comments in their diaries about how often the Boss changes his mind. Private opinions are safe on the page. Expressing such exasperation aloud would be foolhardy. This is not the time to appear disloyal, although they are all deeply disappointed. There are more muttered comments when a nearby crack threatens the camp and everyone has to struggle from bed to move the tents and sledges and wrangle the dogs. The entire world appears against them.

The wake-up call comes early. Seven o'clock is a brutal start for men who didn't get to sleep until one or two in the morning, but the ice they're on does not look solid enough to last. The Boss wants them to retreat even further, and immediately. It's a great pity that as much as the pack ice has softened, the spaces between the floes have not opened up. They are in a no-man's land – neither on a firm footing nor with any real prospects of launching the boats.

The only good thing about not managing to travel any great distance from Ocean Camp is that dog teams can be sent back to retrieve all remaining food supplies. Hurley and

Dr Macklin are happy to go. Macklin is sure there are things worth salvaging that they couldn't face carrying. Hurley's photographic plates are a case in point. At Worsley's urging, another group brings up the third lifeboat.

Despite being reluctant to take on any more pushing and pulling, their effort pays off. Shortly after they return to the new camp, swathes of dark water cut them off from their old home completely. Open leads to the south, ice to the north – the inverse of what is needed. What a cruel irony. The list of injustices keeps growing. It scarcely seems worth shaking one's fist. Resignation seems a more appropriate response after two months of living in the open. It could be worse; they could be dead. Their new base, which has been christened 'Patience Camp', is on a surer footing, a solid, older floe that appears to be a kilometre or so across. It may be home for a while yet.

So much anger has been directed at the lifeboats over the last few days. Cursed repeatedly as dead weight, the three boats have survived the journey over the uneven pack largely unscathed. Now that the men don't need to do any more hauling, all is forgiven. Everybody recognises that these boats will play a central role in their survival. It seems only right that they should have names. Three expedition sponsors will be honoured. The larger of the three is christened the *James Caird*, the two smaller ones will be known as the *Stancomb Wills* and the *Dudley Docker*.

*

There is not much to celebrate on New Year's Eve. Another grey day of snow flurries when the ground and sky merge and the hours pass at a snail's pace. This time last year they were sailing south, full of excitement. There was singing and feasting and carousing in the ship's wardroom, with music warbling out from the gramophone before anyone considered it a cursed object. Clean clothes, round rosy cheeks and freshly shaved faces – those were different men, buoyed by the surge of adventure, not motivated by fear and boredom.

A certain forced frivolity pervades the camp this year. Genuine heartiness is difficult to muster when the final day of 1915 is a poignant reminder of their extended absence from home. Most of the men left their families back in Britain at the beginning of August 1914 – almost a year and a half ago. Hussey's banjo can be heard and snatches of songs echo from the tents, but there won't be a party as such. There is nowhere to gather as a group except out on the ice, and the weather is not conducive to holding open-air celebrations, the slushy surface even less so. The food is not quite up to the same high standard as last year's festive fare. There will be no plum pudding and jugged hare on Green's truncated menu. Despite this, food is still very much the highlight of the day.

'Who would think hard round cakes made from dog food could be so appealing?' says Blackborow, positioning the bannocks on the griddle, his mouth watering.

'Surprisingly versatile ingredient, this dog pemmican,' says Green. He's found it especially handy when it comes to replacing flour in the bannock recipe. 'They may look peculiar, but they smell nice and the taste is perfectly acceptable.'

'Nobody has suggested smearing them with honey or jam yet,' Blackborow says.

Green snorts, 'Believe me, if we had any, they would!'

Now that their supply of flour is almost exhausted, improvisation has become a standard feature of their meals. Sustained by an increasingly meaty diet, their poor bodies cry out for any form of carbohydrate. Bread and scones and potatoes are the stuff of daydreams. The men often lie in their sleeping bags entertaining each other with imaginary afternoon teas involving crisp white rolls and sweet cakes.

Blackborow clutches the warm saucepan to his belly and traipses from tent to tent. Each bannock will be consumed according to individual preference. Some like to wolf meals down before they have a chance to get cold, whatever is on the plate. Those who prefer to savour each mouthful tend to tear the bannock into little squares, while the masters of self-control eat only half, and tuck any leftovers into a pocket or sleeping bag. Just knowing it is there is enough to prolong the enjoyment of consuming even the most meagre morsel.

The only grumbling about the food appearing from the galley relates to quantity. The portions never seem to be large enough to truly satisfy. That their appetites are insatiable should come as no surprise. Their everyday existence has been stripped of all but the simplest pleasures. Hunger, boredom and cold are the only constants, and food is the only thing that fixes all three at once, albeit temporarily.

Green is doing a marvellous job in circumstances more trying than ever. The new camp kitchen is a marvel of inventiveness. Empty provision boxes serve both as storage and makeshift walls and form a sizeable work surface for prepping, while a sailcloth has been rigged up on oars to shelter the cook and his two blubber stoves from the worst of the weather. It is a joy to not have to unload everything from a sledge three times a day. That in itself was a full-time occupation.

While on the march, Orde-Lees was signed up to galley duty, but the experience was far from pleasant – for anyone. It didn't take him long to tire of the greasy soot and smoke. Now that they have a more permanent set-up, Orde-Lees has been relieved of his post, but he has a favour to ask the cook.

'Green, can I have some soap?'

Green shakes his head. He's heard nothing but complaints from Orde-Lees about how filthy the blubber smoke made him. The cook would love to get clean himself; however, washing would be a waste of soap. Green would be back to looking like a chimneysweep by suppertime. 'Ask Greenstreet, I've heard that he has a little bit left.'

Stripped to the waist with a small chunk of Lionel Greenstreet's precious Sunlight soap in hand, Orde-Lees disappears behind the tents and rubs himself all over with snow in a blisteringly cold display of determination. By the end of it, his pale skin is pink with fright, but his face and hands are still covered in grime. Unfortunately, it is the cleanest start to the new year that he will manage in such field conditions. Shivering violently, Orde-Lees returns the soap to its owner.

'Your ablutions weren't exactly effective,' says the sailor.

Orde-Lees sighs. 'That may be, but I won't forget your kindness, Greenstreet.'

In the afternoon, a hunting party sets out across the pack ice with a couple of dog teams. While they can always use extra seal meat, the Boss is getting increasingly agitated at the recklessness shown on such excursions. 'Cautious Jack' now insists that any man leaving camp must be part of a group. Some individuals have been known to disappear for several hours, striking out a bit further every time as they get more blasé about safety. Orde-Lees is a notable offender who frequently heads off for extended jaunts on skis. Hurley is the same.

It's not just the stability of the floes that is at issue; there is also the risk that leads might open up in the pack and cut off whomever has ventured too far afield, without anyone on hand to raise the alarm. Perhaps even more worrying is the fact that the weather is so changeable. Conditions deteriorate swiftly, from perfect visibility to total whiteout in mere minutes. A man could be stumbling around for days in the mists without food or water or any idea where he is.

The hunters return in time for supper with an emperor penguin and six seals loaded on the sledges. They also have an enormous sea leopard displayed like a trophy. It's easily twice the size of a man. There is much excited chatter as Crean and Dr Macklin slice into the creature. Its belly is full of grisly contents – chunks of seal and penguin, fur balls and fermented fish, all of which will be fed to the dogs.

It's the first sea leopard they've seen, and quite terrifying. Wild managed to kill it with a single shot to the head. Not a moment too soon either. Seconds before it had been pursuing Orde-Lees with such speed and vicious intent that it would have had him in its fearsome jaws if he had tipped off his skis. In the past Orde-Lees has found a heavy slap with the edge of a ski enough to stun a seal. It's unlikely that such a technique would prove effective against one of these aggressive creatures. The encounter has certainly left an impression on all the men and made Orde-Lees rethink his wayfaring. Breaking the tedium of camp life is one thing, paying with one's life is another.

CHAPTER FIFTEEN

JANUARY–FEBRUARY 1916

All of January and most of February are spent lying around. Some smoke, some read, some just stare at tent walls and wait until somebody suggests a walk or a game of poker. The playing cards are so dirty they're barely recognisable. It's high time somebody spruced up the pack again so they can at least tell the spades from the clubs, the hearts from the diamonds more easily.

'I'm constipated, Mack.'

Dr Macklin grunts, and peers over the top of his poker hand at the biologist. 'Not much I can do about that, Clark. Our sedentary lifestyle is probably to blame.'

'I suspect all that meat doesn't help me.'

'Well, there are other benefits to eating meat. Not to discount your discomfort, of course.' The doctor places his cards on the blanket that serves as their table. 'But it could be worse.'

Clark scoffs, 'What could possibly be worse than constipation?'

'Piles,' Worsley interjects.

'Actually, I was thinking of something else.' Macklin holds his index finger to his lips.

'What?'

Discretion is needed. The canvas walls may do an adequate job of blocking the southerly gales but a private conversation passes right through them. They have all learnt this lesson the hard way. Dr Macklin mouths the word that nobody would say aloud. The Boss does not like talk of scurvy. It's as if the word itself is enough to conjure up the deadly menace that has stalked mariners and explorers for centuries. Ever since the *Endurance* sank, Dr Macklin and Dr McIlroy have been keeping a close eye on the men. The warning signs are obvious: extreme lethargy, erupting skin and blackened gums. So far, they've been lucky. Although general listlessness and depression are becoming more of a danger.

'Mack, why don't seals and penguins get —?' Orde-Lees mouths the word.

'Nobody knows. There is so much we don't understand about the condition. About prevention or a cure.'

'We had all that lime juice to take on the march across the continent,' says Hudson from his sleeping bag.

'Fat lot of good it does us on the sea floor,' says Worsley.

Dr Macklin clears his throat. 'There are some who believe scurvy is the result of an intestinal toxin which builds up when there is not enough green matter in the diet.'

'There's none in ours!' Worsley snorts. 'I'd be happy to see the colour green. Don't even need to eat it!'

Orde-Lees interrupts, 'We should be eating all parts of the seal and the penguin – brains, heart, liver, kidney and sweetbreads. I'm sure there are benefits to our health. It's a waste giving all those bits to the dogs.'

'Yes, undoubtedly. Eating as widely as possible seems to be a good thing.' Macklin folds his deck. 'I think cleanliness is important too, particularly when it comes to food preparation. And we should avoid constipation at all costs. We must try to keep our systems moving.'

'Can't claim a whole lot of success in that department,' says Clark with a despondent look.

'Not sure we're that successful on the cleanliness front either.' Worsley holds up grimy cards in an even grimier fist and laughs.

'And you can forget about variety, if we're stuck here much longer,' Orde-Lees says primly. 'Once our stores are used up – it'll be penguin, seal and blubber all the way.'

'And it's not already?' grumbles Hudson from his sleeping bag.

Waiting. Waiting. Waiting, Shackleton writes in his diary. He looks at the otherwise blank page. There is simply nothing else to add. He longs for action, for something to report other than all this idleness. His back is killing him, but he won't bother noting that. If he starts enumerating his ills, he'll fill the remaining pages of the diary. *I have seen far worse,* he thinks, lifting himself onto one elbow and contemplating the prospect of stretching his legs. These weeks and months, he has been telling the men the same thing repeatedly: *We shall put the foot of courage into the stirrup of patience.*

Stepping outside, he looks about the scruffy encampment where balding sleeping bags and increasingly threadbare blankets hang limply on a makeshift clothesline or on the end of oars. It's unlikely they will dry out much. The day is windless and raw. There's no sun. The sky is white and flat with a translucence not unlike porcelain. What lies underfoot looks virtually the same, although the sensation of sinking knee-deep into the softening snow makes one feel more shackled to reality than ever. The pack ice is loosening, opening and closing like a creature yawning itself awake. The small leads around their floe contain much brash ice. The day is so quiet he can hear it whispering in the gaps like wind in telegraph wires. Even the dogs are silent. The Boss wonders if they sense the end is coming.

Ruefully, he recalls the months in London leading up to their departure when there were not enough hours in the day. Time seemed to slip through his fingers. Calling in favours and shaking on deals, verifying offers of assistance, wheedling and pleading in a jocular fashion that he hoped would disguise his growing sense of desperation. Often, he would ask the taxi to keep the meter running as he dashed into another sponsor's house, sweat trickling down his neck under his tight-fitting collar and tie. Countless times he said to the driver: *I won't be long.* And now, time stretches out interminably.

Stooping to the door of the neighbouring tent, Shackleton forces a smile and asks, 'Any of you lads got time for a walk?'

Wordie and Chippy are also taking a stroll. They routinely make the tour of the floe, a distance of almost 2 kilometres if one keeps to the periphery. Wordie usually allows himself six or seven circuits a day, sometimes with Dr Macklin or his fellow scientists but most often with Chippy. The carpenter and the geologist are as odd a pairing as Hurley and Jimmy, but there is genuine affection between the two Scotsmen. They stare out over the undulating fields of fractured floes and wonder how they will ever escape the icy maze.

Chippy nurses the usual gripes, chief among them being the discomfort of an empty stomach. Seals are in short supply, which has implications for the food situation as well as fuel supply. They're down to one hot drink a day – a cup of tea at breakfast-time, while supplies last. Coffee is a thing of the past. At lunch and supper, there's only cold water.

'What I wouldn't do for a cup of hot milk,' Chippy says. 'There seems to be plenty of milk powder, but Green says he hasn't the blubber to warm the water.'

'I'd like that too,' Wordie mumbles. The longing for liquids is a new form of torture. Hot drinks are one thing, but there never even seems to be enough water. Some of the men have taken to packing snow into a tobacco tin at night. By placing it between two layers of clothing, it has a chance to thaw. It lowers the body temperature but at least on waking there is something to drink.

Wordie pauses. 'How many hours until supper?'

'Too many,' says Chippy. 'Nothing for it but to get into the sleeping bag and smoke away the hunger.'

Wordie thinks of his pouch of tobacco, mostly intact, kept in reserve. It might be needed later. Food is not so easy to put aside, although plenty of men do keep a little stash of things to nibble on. Some have even started to trade comestibles. Try as he might, the geologist cannot resist the lure of immediate gratification.

Their conversation is interrupted by the crack of Wild's rifle. The reports continue to echo across the floes, ten seconds or so apart. Both men feel a pang of excitement at the thought of fresh seal meat. Then they remember that, in this instance, the sound of Wild's firearm has nothing to do with the hunt. The cull has commenced.

Not all the dogs will be destroyed at once. It will be a process of gradual attrition. With appetites as ravenous as ever, the animals chew through meat at an alarming rate. The dogs brought a certain liveliness to Patience Camp. There is not one man who does not regret their apparent expendability after all their hard work and loyalty, but it's inevitable; they simply cannot sustain the animals and themselves with their limited supplies of meat. Most of the dogs have pulled their last.

'Lord Almighty,' breathes Chippy.

'I wonder how the dog meat will taste,' murmurs Wordie.

CHAPTER SIXTEEN

MARCH 1916

Orde-Lees wants to vomit. With aching guts, he rolls onto his back, closes his eyes and wishes the nausea away. Sleep will not return. He feels so wretched. He hasn't felt like this in months. In fact, it's a sensation he hasn't experienced since the sea crossing from England. *Aha!* the thought suddenly pops into his head.

'I'm seasick!' he hollers with excitement. 'I'm seasick.'

The revelation is met with grunts from his groggy tent mates. Gleefully Orde-Lees extracts himself from his sleeping bag and stumbles out into the daylight. The pack ice offers not a hint of movement. But Orde-Lees knows what he feels and off he dashes to report his malaise to the Boss. Shackleton breathes deeply and smiles. He doesn't dare say that this might be the moment they've been waiting for – the final breaking up of the pack. He's been wrong before.

Worsley and Wild are alerted. The captain is certain Orde-Lees is correct. He stands stock-still for a long time observing the horizon, feeling the floe through his feet. 'He's right,' he says. 'Open water can't be far off.'

Wild is less sanguine. It is good news, no doubt. But aren't they forgetting? The outer edge of the pack is a churning battleground, a zone of calamity where ice and ocean clash, where chunks of floe and the severed sides of icebergs weighing hundreds of tonnes smash themselves to bits in one final frenzy. He's dreading the time when they take to the boats. Far preferable to drift as far as they can on a disintegrating ice floe than take to the water and face the conditions seafarers dread most.

Lifeboats are stacked with clothing and supplies and ice is cleared from the sledge runners so they can be hauled into position at a moment's notice. Wild looks at their three frail boats, and wishes they were better prepared.

Nervous chatter echoes through the tents and the men go to sleep fully clothed, boots at the ready. The night watch is reinstated. Two men shelter from the wind in the lee of the galley and smoke and chat about finally commencing the next stage in their homeward journey. But there is nothing to report the following morning. Or for several days. A week passes. There is nothing to do but wait. Orde-Lees wonders if it was all in his head. A case of wishful nausea.

Captain Worsley watches the horizon anxiously. Every day he clambers atop a nearby chunk of ice that offers greater elevation and peers into the murk for any sight of land.

'Mt Haddington!' he cries more than once.

Nobody takes much notice anymore. Refusing to be discouraged, Worsley continues his lonely vigil in all weathers, straining his eyes, hoping his hours of cold surveillance will finally pay off. But there is nothing to see. As diligent as ever in his meteorological readings, Hussey reports daily on wind direction, while Worsley checks on their rate of drift; neither appear satisfactory to the men who wait so avidly for action.

In the doldrums-like existence, books no longer offer much escape. They've all been read anyway. Conversation has been replaced by monosyllabic exchanges. The days are getting shorter. One good thing is they can sleep longer, but the temperature is also dropping. Breath escapes in white clouds, even inside the tents. One morning a layer of ice forms on the top of a pot of water before the occupants have a chance to take a drink. It is brutally cold. It is autumn.

Whenever they are spotted, penguins are rounded up for the slaughter. Sometimes a seal is caught close to a breathing hole. But there's never enough meat and blubber to get the men back onto full rations. Breakfast is dog pemmican, thawed for the morning in some unlucky man's sleeping bag overnight so it can be cut up and added to each man's mug of tepid water. Lunch is a biscuit and six lumps of sugar. The evening meal consists of a meagre helping of meat, followed by a pipe. Conversation is muted. Ears that were forever seeking the sound of lapping water now only hear the play of wind and snow on canvas. Perhaps they can persuade Hussey to get his banjo out again after all. Perhaps he can learn a few new songs, as the old ones are getting a bit stale.

Curse this inaction, seethes Shackleton inwardly. He keeps his frustrations to himself. Outwardly he's the very image of courage and resilience.

'Mt Haddington!' Worsley shouts again.

This time the captain is not the only one to see the outline. It looks to be the very tip of the Antarctic Peninsula. A few pessimists still believe it to be clouds massing on the horizon, but after a few tense hours, it becomes clear as day. Breath-holding turns to cheering. They're approaching the end of March 1916. It is their first sight of land since January 1915.

Even though it is closer, Paulet Island is small and not yet discernible through the mists that hover over the sea ice.

Worsley estimates it to be less than 100 kilometres to the west. The state of the pack ice makes the island completely inaccessible. The surface is fractured and slushy – to strike out from their solid floe on foot would be suicide. Neither can they launch the boats – there's no open water to speak of; at best it's a chunky, soupy mess. To have drifted so far north is marvellous, but when Worsley takes a sighting, he realises that they are also being carried eastward, away from land. Moreover, their floe is at risk of being caught in the swirl of clockwise currents that describe the outside edge of the Weddell Sea – a zone of broken bergs and massive swells. To end up there would be Frank Wild's worst nightmare – a veritable meat grinder for small boats.

Unable to do anything at all, the men surrender to the drift eastward. By late March there are few developments, only more setbacks. The weather is stormy. The southerly gales make it almost too cold to sleep.

The men are hungrier than ever. Vincent and a couple of others pilfer some scraps of blubber to gnaw on in the secrecy of their tent. It's a pathetic haul, more scavenging than thievery. Nobody would have considered eating raw offcuts a few months ago; they would have gagged. When discovered, their petty crime is a cause for consternation. Shackleton gives them a full dressing-down, then sends Dr Macklin to sift through the same pile of galley waste to see if other morsels can be salvaged. Heads and flippers, odds and ends, it's revolting gunge and some of it reeks. In the past it would have been considered fit only for dogs. Now, it's slated for human consumption. Green will disguise it as best he can. Nobody mentions the cached food supplies left by Nordenskjöld's shipwrecked crew on Paulet Island. The longed-for Swedish provisions might as well be stashed on the moon.

'If we've drifted out of range of Paulet Island, better try for the South Shetlands,' says Worsley, spreading his chart in front of Shackleton and Wild. 'There are a dozen or so islands in the group. Deception is probably our best bet.' Worsley points to the horseshoe-shaped island. 'The whalers use it as a safe anchorage when the weather is bad. Sure to be supplies cached ashore. I've heard the whalers built a little wooden church there.'

The Boss nods slowly. 'If we needed to, we could use the wood from the church to build a bigger boat, something more suited to an ocean crossing than the lifeboats.'

'That's if we don't encounter anybody there,' says Wild.

'What are the chances?' Shackleton asks.

Worsley frowns and stares down at the map. 'Well, the whaling season is over already. At the very least, we'll need to wait until the end of the year. November maybe? But who's to say any ships will call in there? No guarantees.'

'If we can get food there, then it's worth it.'

'SIR ERNEST'

NIMROD EXPEDITION 1909

Euphoria comes in bites. The first pang of air on exiting the tent, a glance upwards on the march that jolts a man from his private thoughts to see this place as if for the first time, so magnificent and strange. These are moments when Shackleton longs to capture the poetry at world's end. Then there are periods when the strange place mocks them with its throbbing whiteness, the infinity of its undulating surface. It wants to cripple the men, to rob them of sight and even the language to describe the vileness of their situation.

The four men lean into the headwind through sour days of slow progress and allow the cheerfulness of their comrades to carry them ever onward. Already they have achieved the impossible – they have ascended the Beardmore Glacier.

'It is the only thing to do for we must get to the Pole, come what may . . .' Shackleton's pencil hovers over the last words in his diary. Come what may? To reach the pole and die, or abandon their quest and survive? His gaze falls on his tent mates, Wild and Adams and Marshall, as they commit their own words to paper in the cold night. He crosses out the last part. It's not worth dying.

Can there be any hope of making a final push across the polar plateau with hunger crowding their every thought and altitude making even the act of breathing a trial? Every so often, Shackleton calls a halt to their march and they lie down on the snow, panting and counting. Three minutes' rest is all. They regain their breath and resist the temptation to stay where they are, laid out like corpses. Chances are, they can squeeze another three days from a week's ration-bag, but they cannot spin out their food indefinitely. It's as if they are swimming further and further from shore, testing the limits of their mental and physical toughness, but the men are spent. Shackleton has headaches and dizzy spells. Can they trust themselves to leave enough in reserve for the return journey while pushing themselves for one last day?

Hot food cannot completely restore warmth but it eradicates the cramps for long enough to get them moving at four o'clock in the morning, all white breath and crunching footfalls. They carry with them nothing but essentials – the Union Jack (the heavy silk one Frank Wild has slept with wrapped around him), some chocolate, *a few biscuits. This is to be the final dash, on legs that have been emptied of all vigour. Still, they give it everything – a final five hours of progress is a fine achievement. They have not reached the South Pole but they have beaten the furthest south record, the one set by Scott, Wilson and Shackleton himself in 1903. They've beaten it by 589 kilometres. It's not a moment to savour. They plant the flag, turn on their heels and flee. Only death lies ahead.*

The way back is unbearable. There's nothing to grip to on wind-stripped ice. They fall heavily on the blue, slick surface as they try to arrest the sideways slide of their runaway sledge on the glacier. If they weren't so wretched they might laugh at their inexpert flailing, at the comedy of the situation. After doing more than his share of the work, Shackleton is ill and cannot eat. He is snow-blind, his eyes full of sharp sand, his lids squeezing themselves closed against his will. His reedy limbs are bruised black and his heels have cracked open in four places.

'How does the Boss carry on?' Wild asks.

Only then do they come to the worst part. Terrain unbound by any laws. Rough, crevassed, cryptic sections that cannot be negotiated. Biscuits finished, sugar gone. Shaking with hunger, their gait is more akin to toppling over. Down and down and bloody down the glacier. Forty hours without solid food, holes ripped in their Burberry suits where the cold can gain yet more purchase on their wizened frames, which scarcely look human. The last insult is for Shackleton alone. The Beardmore snags him, flicking his body into a crevasse, wide like a mouth thrown open in laughter. His harness catches him under the heart with a sudden jag of pain and he's coughing and coughing and once again he's in the tent with Scott and Wilson and he's almost dying and for a split second he wishes it would all be over.

And then, it is. Headlines and parades and celebratory dinners displace the memory of coughing, of cold and hunger and the infinite placing of one foot in front of the other. Held aloft by strangers in foreign cities, Ernest Shackleton has never clasped so many hands. Everyone wants to congratulate him, bask in his reflected glory, join him on his next escapade and nobody cares what it is. Caught in a blizzard at world's end in January, invested with a knighthood at Buckingham Palace in December; Shackleton scarcely has time to take it all in.

'Arise, Sir Ernest.'

PART III

COURAGE

CHAPTER SEVENTEEN

APRIL 1916

'Crack!' the watchman shouts in the dead of night.

It has become a bit of a catchcry by the second week of April. Action of any kind sets the heart racing and breaks the tedium, but this time the massive crack splits the camp, almost down the middle. Perhaps this is the moment they have been anticipating for long weeks.

'Move it, lads!' The Boss's exuberance is contagious.

The men work swiftly. A few brave fellows leap over the widening gap of water to rescue meat and provisions, tossing boxes to comrades across the lead. Nobody goes back to bed.

Breathless, they stand around until night becomes day. Their home is cut in half once more. It's halved again before lunchtime until there's barely enough room on the floe for men and boats. Suddenly it's obvious what needs to happen next.

The wind is picking up when Shackleton finally gives the order to launch the boats, in a calm and clear voice that belies his trepidation. Polar exploration is where he is most at home; on the ice is where he is confident of keeping men safe. Navigating open water is another kettle of fish.

The *Dudley Docker* is first away. The smallest of the boats, the *Docker* is packed to the gunwales with boxes, canvas-wrapped seal meat and blubber, a Primus stove and sundry supplies. Worsley stands in the stern well and assigns places to his crew of eight. When the sailor Ernie Holness answers an order with 'Yes Captain', he can't help but smile. It's been almost six months since he commanded a crew.

Orde-Lees is not so happy to be on the water. Seasick again, he must contend with a heaving stomach. The rise and fall of the swell is amplified in the small boat. He barely has time to position his head over the side. A spray of vomit is pitched back by the wind, splattering across the assorted cargo.

'Curse you, Lees!'

'Never throw up to windward, you halfwit!'

'Imbecile!' The other men don't hold back. Orde-Lees is unpopular at the best of times, but with nervous tension running at an all-time high, the abuse comes thick and fast.

Dr Macklin shelters his medical kit from the wind-whipped sea spray. There's nothing in it to offer those feeling queasy – it's not just Orde-Lees. The scientists seem far from cheerful at the oars. They look about apprehensively as they help manoeuvre the boat out into the widening channel between the floes. They're in a zone of mess and violence. The edges of the pack hammer together with enough force to take off a man's leg. It will make matchsticks of their little boat if they don't get away. Nobody has had any practice rowing in open water, least of all working in concert. The sailors Holness and McLeod look more at home at the rowlock and establish a rhythm they hope the scientists can manage. A prolonged stay on 'dry land' was not what either of them had bargained for when they signed up to the voyage. At last a return to seafaring! Neither man cares that the *Dudley Docker* is nothing more than a glorified dinghy, fairly suited for weekend coastal sailing but not robust enough for open seas. They feel liberated.

'This boat handles like a bad-tempered mule,' Worsley complains. 'Swap yourselves around so we're more balanced.'

'That wretched thing isn't helping us any,' says Holness, gesturing with his head at the sledge dragging behind the boat on the end of a tether. An insurance policy. In case their journey takes them overland. It was the Boss's idea, but the way it snags on every knuckle of ice and tugs them continually off course, the sledge is a mighty hindrance.

'Well, I won't have it,' says Worsley, irritated. One flick of his pocketknife and they're free.

The sledge looks oddly forlorn, tossing on the ice-strewn water. If plans had not gone so awry, it would have crossed the Antarctic continent by now. Who knows where the ocean swell will take it? All eyes watch it compete with the rise and fall of the broken pack.

Hudson is the skipper of the smallest of the boats, the *Stancomb Wills*. Drifting these past months has been a mental struggle for a navigator. It's more than a year since the *Endurance* was caught in the pack ice. To be back at his shipboard duties will give him a boost. At least the Boss hopes he'll perk up. Tom Crean is not so sure. Hudson isn't ready to take the helm, or responsibility for other people's safety. Crean can tell that he'll need bolstering. Shackleton has clearly paired them up for that reason. Crean may shun leadership but the Irishman is truly unflappable and the more experienced man.

Hudson and Crean and their crew of six have a fair-sized challenge on their hands. *Stancomb Wills* is the least suited to open seas. Keeping pace will be an issue. Its sails are far too small for its size and it is hopelessly overloaded. The *Wills* doesn't sit much above the waterline. As soon as it's launched, the boat is shipping icy water over the side. Seasoned sailors Bakewell, How and Stephenson barely register the fact that their feet and legs are already wet through. Blackborow does. He winces as the freezing sea water permeates his boots. Working alongside the three sailors at the rowlocks, Blackborow is soon warm, his upper body buzzing with this new form of exertion. He grips his oar as the boat jerks and tips with an unfamiliar cadence. He's more than a little apprehensive and wishes he could see the other men's faces. He could use some reassurance.

'We're going to need to row like hell to escape this mess,' Bakewell says.

Finally, with the other two boats waiting at a safe distance, Shackleton gives the order for the *James Caird* to be launched. A final heave and the largest lifeboat is over the ice edge and into the turbulent water. It too is overladen, but perhaps more of a concern for Shackleton is the cargo of diffi-cult personalities. For this reason alone, he has opted to have Wild with him. Vincent and Chippy are already bickering. Having painstakingly built up the gunwales using timbers from the *Endurance*, the carpenter realises that the seats are now too low to grip the oars comfortably. The first strokes in the water are awkward and ineffectual, the angle quite wrong for efficient handling. Vincent squares his shoulders with his arms high in front of him and tries again. The other oarsmen are having similar trouble. Vincent swears. How he'd love to bash the carpenter with one of the useless-seeming oars.

Their most pressing need is to get to open water before darkness descends. Shackleton stands in the cockpit and pilots the *Caird* out in front, picking a path through the ice-choked labyrinth while the other two boats keep up as best they can. The Boss turns repeatedly to check their progress. Expecting to see the pack recede, he's horrified. It seems to chase them. The further they pull away, the faster it gains on them. The wind and currents carry it forward with such momentum that a bow wave swells before it as though it were a warship at full steam. Not until nightfall do they finally outrun it.

The water around them is a jumble of ice at various stages of destruction, rising and falling with each movement of the waves. Some larger floes stand proud, a foot or more above the wash, while plenty of smaller blocks of ice float by looking soft and woolly as they melt. By five o'clock it's getting dark. While they appear to be through the worst, the Boss thinks it best to call a halt. A solid-looking berg offers enough of a flat surface to pitch tents and cook some supper, although it's moving about in the swell a fair bit. A seal blinks at the men as they secure the boats. They fall on the poor creature and have it butchered before Green has finished setting up his cooking gear. Despite their stolid feed, the men are rattled by the day's strenuous new rhythm. It's extremely cold and they're in unfamiliar surroundings. Rest does not come easily. There's also the anxiety about their prospects. The idea of sheltering on an island of ice surrounded by deep ocean is enough to keep many of them on tenterhooks all night. And just as well. When a large crack opens directly under one of the tents, there are plenty of men to sound the alarm. Amid the general scramble in the dark, there's sudden shouting.

'Ernie's in the water!'

Trapped in his sleeping bag, Ernie Holness wrestles one arm free and flails about for a handhold while his dark hair twists in slow motion below the surface. Grabbing his collar and a sleeve, the Boss somehow finds the strength to haul him out, wringing wet and triple his normal weight. The precious sleeping bag, dense as a sack of cement, is flopped onto the floe beside him just as the jaws of ice slam back together. Too shocked to thank his rescuer, Holness starts to shake. It is as if electricity has taken possession of his body.

'Get him up. Keep him moving.' The Boss's wet hands throb once they come in contact with the air. It must be minus 20 at least. And his sleeves, wet to the elbow, have started to freeze. He fumbles his fists into his mitts.

Holness whimpers in feeble snatches. 'My 'baccy. It was in my pocket.'

The other sailors reassure him. They promise to share their own dwindling tobacco supplies as they march him back and forth, his increasingly brittle clothing creaking and crackling as it turns to ice. It's not clear anymore if he's shaking with cold or with the anguish of having lost the only thing that gave pleasure.

Vincent scolds him. 'You should be pleased to be alive, Ernie!'

'Keep him walking!' calls Shackleton again, this time more sternly.

When a new crack appears, the scene is plunged into chaos. The men leap over in twos and threes to join the others until the only man stranded is the Boss. The gap widens to a several metres. Wild throws him a rope, but it falls short and the current whisks the floes apart at terrific speed. Shackleton watches with growing alarm. He's being carried out to sea. He forgets his frozen hands. All he is aware of is the thumping in his chest and the dark outlines of his men becoming smaller in the half-light.

Come on, Wild, don't abandon me now, he thinks.

Rowers are dispatched before Shackleton is completely lost from view. Nobody dares speak until he's safely back among them.

Wild clasps the Boss's shoulders. 'Make sure you take some food next time you try to get away.'

All thoughts of camping are abandoned. It's too dangerous. Their second night is spent in the boats, tethered to a crumbling floe. Only Green clambers out of the *Docker* to cook a meagre supper over the Primus before climbing back aboard with the others. It's a night of high anxiety. Subject to a barrage of waves, their temporary anchorage is far from restful.

From now on, the only safe option will be to lash together and drift during the night on the open sea. Cooking in the conventional sense will need to be abandoned too. There is no room in any of the boats to cook over a naked flame. Better make do with whatever can be eaten uncooked. They'll jettison half their provisions to lighten the boats and create a little more space. Every movement of bodies requires careful choreography, shuffling of bottoms and crawling over each other and rearranging legs and arms amid the pitch and roll and sprays of water. Tempers flare. There is even less room than in their old tents.

A break in the weather would enable Worsley to take sightings, establish their position more accurately. Relying on dead-reckoning is a risky business. Worsley had been convinced that they lay at 55 degrees west but their longitude is off. They're too far east. And by a significant margin. His last sextant reading puts them a depressing distance from their destination. It's not that they've made little headway towards Deception Island, they are further away than when they started. The South Shetlands now look completely unattainable. First Paulet, now the South Shetlands. It's depressing news to greet Shackleton with when he climbs aboard the *Dudley Docker* to confer with Worsley.

'Don't tell anyone,' the Boss whispers as he folds the chart.

Worsley understands completely. Do they continue to fight their way west even as the powerful currents push them further east? Another suggestion is Hope Bay. It lies to the south-west of their position, but it is so far off the beaten track as to be useless. Whaling ships do not frequent such remote areas. What would be the point? Options are few. The boats are tending northward. If they allow foul winds to dictate their course then they could consider landing at Elephant Island or its neighbour Clarence Island. Two dots on the map, the islands still lie 80 kilometres away. If they're lucky, the weather will continue to offer a helping hand. But if visibility is poor, they might overshoot or be swept between the two islands, in which case the only thing beyond is the vast emptiness of the South Atlantic.

'If we get our bearings wrong, we'll be finished.'

'Then we shall not get our bearings wrong, Skipper. Will we?'

The evening of their third night huddled in the boats is the most unpleasant yet. Choppy seas batter them from every direction and icy sea spray trickles down into their sodden clothing that was never intended as wet-weather gear. The whitecaps stretch out in infinite ranks. Every so often darker waves gather to ominous liquid peaks and crash down on their cowering heads. Everywhere they look, there is water. If only it was the kind to slake one's thirst. It seems ridiculous that nobody thought to bring fresh water or even ice to melt.

Orde-Lees is no longer the only man suffering seasickness. Others feel their guts twist with nausea. A few have diarrhoea from consuming uncooked dog pemmican. They sling their rear ends over the gunwales and brace for the nasty slap of freezing sea water on bare skin. Just when things cannot possibly get worse, the killer whales start to gather. The sound of them surfacing close by and in such numbers is terrifying – even more so at night. It is the stuff of nightmares.

'Evil creatures,' Chippy hisses.

'Come to see if they can finish us off,' somebody else suggests.

'As if we need any help,' Hurley mutters. 'We seem to be doing perfectly well on our own.'

CHAPTER EIGHTEEN

APRIL 1916

Blackborow opens his mouth to the sky. Sleet has been raining down on them since the wee small hours. Blown about on the light breeze in chaotic swirls, little of it lands on his parched tongue. Instead it sticks to his face and cracked lips and only makes him colder.

They've woken to a strange sight this morning. The sea is motionless, caught under a fragile glaze of fine white ice. The oars are covered too. Everything is locked in place under layers of frozen sleet. The weight of it is considerable and the bow dips unnaturally towards the waterline. There must be a quarter of a tonne or more of it loading down the boat. A volunteer shimmies along the decking to see if he can chip the ice off. Before he knows what is happening, he's sliding. There's a splash and shouting and then panicked shrieking as though he's been dropped in scalding water. When he's dragged back on board, he sets the whole boat vibrating.

The cold is penetrating. It strips them of language and the ability to sleep and steals even their memory of what it feels like to be warm. Sheltering under ice-stiffened canvas, a few try to make sense of it by asking Hussey what he thinks the temperature might be, but conversations about the cold never end well.

'I don't know how cold it is!' says the meteorologist.

'Then guess!'

'Does it matter?'

'Yes it does.'

'Minus ten.'

'Damn you.'

Hussey is sick of being blamed for the biting weather. In much the same way, Worsley is routinely blamed for their position. The men have ceased to think about things rationally. Their lives have collapsed into the present moment. Being thirsty and freezing and doused by waves.

The level of despair and discontent is much the same on the *Dudley Docker*. Worsley has been at the tiller for three days without a break, eyes fixed on his compass and the sails. But he's terrified of losing sight of the other boats in the mountainous swell. He's the only man skilled enough to keep up with the *Caird*. The exhausted men's heads loll forward then jerk back painfully whenever they're not at the oars. If only there was room to lie down, they would sleep for a year!

Orde-Lees is limp from vomiting. He says he wishes he were dead. Others see his helplessness as laziness. Every time it is his turn to row, he fumbles about with such incompetence that somebody else has to take his turn. Accusations of selfishness rain down on him as he scuttles back to his corner. Nobody believes it when he offers to warm up Greenstreet's frostbitten feet by placing them on his bare belly.

In the *Stancomb Wills*, Hudson has relinquished command to Tom Crean, admitting to the Irishman that it's all too much. For several days their boat has been towed, first by the *Dudley Docker*, then by the *James Caird*. The little boat cannot keep up otherwise. Hudson's hands are frostbitten but it's ultimately the excruciating pain of a boil on his backside that makes sitting at the helm impossible. Hudson eases himself down on his side among the chaos of ice-etched boxes. The waves begin to slosh over him but he is beyond caring. Hudson's apparent mental collapse unnerves the others; one or two seem close to giving up. Even with their boots submerged under near-freezing water, they need reminding to bail. It's as if they have lost their reason.

A couple of men, desperate for fresh water, attempt to haul a sizeable iceblock into the boat.

'Leave it,' Crean chides.

He knows they want to lick away their thirst but they're more likely to fall overboard. Crean doesn't have the strength to pull the foolish wretches out.

'How are you going, lad?' Crean asks Blackborow. 'Make sure you wiggle your toes. Keep the blood moving.'

Blackborow looks up. 'How can I wiggle them if I can't feel them?' The young man would like to cry but he's too dehydrated to produce tears. His feet feel quite dead. Supporting his own weight has become impossible. Nobody asks him to swap places anymore and rowing is out of the question.

By the end of their fourth day, the men are desperate for warmth, fluid, sleep, shelter, any form of sustenance. Those who can stomach it chew the frozen strips of seal blubber from the provision bags but after a time the salty fat only intensifies their thirst. They stare at the waves and the sky with hearts full of hatred. If only they had the strength to hoist themselves over the gunwales, they could pitch their frozen bodies into the sea and it would all be over.

Shackleton looks at the crumpled forms of the men aboard the *James Caird* and wonders how many will survive the journey. Frank Wild harbours the same fear. Stoic as ever, Wild remains at the tiller with the occasional upwards glance at the mainsail. Only his body language betrays how daunted he feels – shoulders drawn up towards his ears, arms held tight by his sides – but he has yet to utter a word of complaint.

Vincent bites down on a sledging biscuit, but his saliva is thicker than glue. He'd have more luck swallowing a mouthful of sawdust. The sharp edges have split his lower lip. He can taste only blood. He spits over the side in disgust. The boat crests a wave as he turns around, throwing him off balance. He collides heavily with another man, whose hands jerk out reflexively to push him away. Grabbing Vincent by the jacket, Shackleton manoeuvres the seaman back into a sitting position at the precise moment that they slip into the trough of a wave. This time it's the Boss who lurches forward, his hands pressed firmly against Vincent's chest for the briefest moment. But it's long enough to feel the object in his breast pocket.

'What've you got in there?' Shackleton says sharply.

Vincent looks blank.

Shackleton stabs a finger at Vincent's chest. 'There.'

Vincent wipes the remaining biscuit crumbs from his scraggly beard. The second's hesitation is a dead giveaway. Shackleton rips open the man's jacket. He pulls out the watch. It takes a moment to register. How did his gold watch end up here, when he had made a point of burying it in the snow all those months ago? He stares at it until he can contain his fury no more.

Vincent lifts his hands to either side of his head as though expecting a fist. His instinct is to pull away but the more he tries, the tighter the hold on his shoulders. A tongue-lashing is all his receives, although Shackleton feels capable of a lot worse.

Releasing his grip, he pushes Vincent roughly to one side and says, 'You shall not have it.'

And with that, there is a flash of gold. All eyes follow the arc of the watch as it sails through the air and disappears into the steely blue ocean with barely a splash. Vincent shifts on his seat, his lips pressed firmly together. Refusing to look at the Boss, he folds his arms across his chest and sinks back into his frozen clothing like a scolded child.

CHAPTER NINETEEN

APRIL 1916

Few men have the strength to summon much enthusiasm when land is spotted on the morning of their fifth day at sea – particularly as the horizon is washed with delicate pinks and reds, a warning of foul weather. Elephant Island is their goal. Logic holds that if they're swept past Elephant, there's still a chance to aim for Clarence Island, its neighbour.

The islands are exactly where Worsley said they would be. It's a major triumph to have pinpointed their location so accurately. Nobody feels the need to congratulate him on his phenomenal navigation skills. A few hours' sleep is his ultimate reward. The challenge will be to move him from his seat at the tiller, where he has remained hunched for days. His body has forgotten any other position. His muscles protest, respond with painful cramps. Greenstreet takes over at the helm. His feet are much better after benefiting from the care and attention of Orde-Lees, who reminded him of a similar kindness involving Sunlight soap. Suddenly he's not viewed with such contempt.

A day's sailing should be all it takes. They could land on Elephant Island by nightfall. The name conjures up all sorts of images in the men's minds. They desperately need water, but they also long to stretch out like human beings after almost a week of perching like chickens. They talk about the luxury of solid ground, lighting a fire to warm their bodies and dry their clothes and feet and melt ice for hoosh. And to cap it all off, a decent night's sleep under canvas, out of reach of the sea spray and squalls. All of it a mere 40 kilometres away.

Nobody notices the island disappear from view behind a dense mist. Greenstreet looks from compass to horizon but he no longer has any point of reference. The wind has also picked up. To be this close and blown off course would be a tragedy, one Greenstreet does not want to be responsible for causing.

'Wake the captain,' he says. 'I don't know where I should steer anymore.'

Rousing calls are ineffective. Orde-Lees gives his shoulder a gentle shake.

'Wake him up, I said.' A note of nervousness enters Greenstreet's voice.

'He won't wake up,' says Orde-Lees.

'What do you mean?' says Greenstreet. 'He has to!'

Others shake the captain more vigorously. A hand presses to his cheek, his frigid forehead. 'Doc, I think he's dead!'

Dr Macklin winces as he eases himself onto his knees amid the brine sloshing about the bottom of the boat. He takes off his mitts and slips his index and middle fingers beneath the layers of damp fabric wound around Worsley's neck. After a moment he gives a nod. 'He's alive.'

'Then why won't he wake up?' Greenstreet's alarm turns quickly to anger.

Dr Macklin growls. 'Because the poor man has been at the tiller for three and a half days without a moment's rest!'

'I don't care!' Greenstreet shouts. 'Wake him up. I can't see where I'm going. We'll be blown off course.'

Shouting has no effect. Shaking is equally ineffectual. Finally, Thomas McLeod delivers a kick to the skipper's head.

'He's awake,' murmurs Orde-Lees. 'Let's hope he can think straight.'

*

As the light fades, the boats are still well off the coast. They need a safe landing spot but visibility is going. Better to take down the sails and ride out the swell overnight a fair distance out to sea than risk heading any closer in the pitch dark. Untold perils lurk in the shallows.

Nobody feels the disappointment more keenly than Shackleton. Their ordeal is endless. Luck seems never to be on their side. Shackleton calls over to the *Stancomb Wills* to check they're all okay, but the rising gale whisks away his words. Tucked out of the wind as best he can in the stern of the little boat, Tom Crean responds with a generous sweep of his arm. His pipe glows red in the dusk. How he managed to light a match is anyone's guess.

The Boss scans the ocean for the *Dudley Docker*. The boat is nowhere to be seen, but it's too early to register concern. Worsley has proven himself time and again to be the most skilled of skippers. But as dependable and indispensable Worsley has become, the Boss will not sleep until they are out of danger, every boat, every single man.

The night is their bleakest yet. Perhaps it is just the bitter irony of imagining a shore that they cannot reach that deadens their spirits. The disappearance of their comrades fills the men with a dread that draws out the night hours, minute by miserable minute. Captain Worsley and Dr Macklin, Greenstreet, Cheetham and Kerr, Marston, Ernie Holness and Thomas McLeod – where are they? And

Orde-Lees? Infuriating as the man may be, nobody wants to imagine him dashed on the rocks. When dawn finally breaks, there is still no sign of the *Docker*. It is the morning of their sixth day in the boats.

Daylight reveals the true nature of Elephant Island. It is a horror of a place. Sheer cliffs, crashing surf, screeching birds, more snow and ice. A dark ribbon of beach comes into view as the boats approach the island. Landing will not be easy. The swell still presents a problem. Surf pounds the shore with the sort of deadly force that worries even the hardiest seamen, but they must get ashore. The men must get something to drink. Rowers manoeuvre the *James Caird* alongside the *Stancomb Wills* and the boats are hurriedly lashed so Shackleton can climb aboard. With Hudson at his wits' end, Tom Crean will need help piloting the most unstable of the lifeboats to shore. None of the others are mentally up to the challenge, although four of them still seem capable of a certain robotic action at the oars that will carry them forward through the breakers.

'Let's give Blackborow the honours,' Shackleton tells the anxious-looking men with a wink. 'First man ashore on Elephant Island. Lad, are you ready?'

The young man looks up at the Boss and tries to smile, but a grimace is all he manages.

'Hold on!' says Crean over the sound of the surf. 'She'll want to tip.'

Once the *Wills* is scooped up by the waves and flung forward, there's precious little anyone can do to alter their course. One last surge carries the *Wills* bow-first onto the pebbled beach.

'Come on lad, off you go!'

Blackborow rises to his feet. Suddenly unstable, he grabs the side of the boat and crumples back onto his seat. Reading his helplessness as hesitation, Shackleton manhandles the boy up and over the side. He lands with a splash on his rump, the waves breaking over his head.

'His feet!' shouts Dr McIlroy. 'The boy can't stand.'

Shackleton leaps to his aid. The young man is spluttering as he carries him free of the waves. It's a marvel he has found the strength.

'Let's just say you're the first to *sit* on Elephant Island,' he says, plonking the young man on the beach and returning to help Crean steady the boat and get the others to safety.

Frank Wild draws level in the *James Caird*. Men spill over the side like rats. Thigh-deep, they wade through the wash and fling themselves onto the wet and glistening shore. Some sink to their knees and lift handfuls of pebbles like precious loot. There's hugging and hopping and laughter that rips their swollen lips into wide smiles. Further up the beach there is plentiful ice to melt for water. Hurley struggles ashore with his photographic plates held high above his head. The cook trudges along the narrow beach gripping an oar, intent on bagging the two seals slumbering just above the high tide mark. Others, inspired by his resolve, get stuck in too. An impromptu flensing operation begins at once.

By the time Worsley and his crew appear from around the headland, the blubber stove is billowing smoke. Reaching shore in time for a drink of hot milk, the crew of the *Dudley Docker* can scarcely believe their ordeal is over. To be having lunch in such surroundings, with seabirds circling overhead, feels outlandish. Seal steaks fried in blubber never tasted so good.

Few, if any, men give thought to what comes next. They have reached their goal. Immediate needs are met. At some point their euphoria will be overtaken by exhaustion. Nobody feels the need to make any predictions or plans, only to collapse and enjoy their first night's rest stretched full length on solid ground.

Sleep is not something the Boss can contemplate just yet. Evidently something is troubling him. He's walked the length of the beach and stands apart as though lost in thought. Hurley joins him.

'It's a deathtrap,' Shackleton says. 'In a gale, we wouldn't last a minute.'

'You're right. Those cliffs. You wouldn't be climbing them in a hurry.'

Worsley and Wild join them. They too can see the beach is too narrow to allow them to establish a more permanent refuge. There are clear signs that the waves have washed the base of the cliffs.

'What do you propose?' Worsley asks wearily.

Wild speaks first. 'I'd be happy to scout another campsite. There may be something along the coast.'

'Are you okay to hop in the boat again, Frank?' asks the Boss with a sigh, although he already knows the answer.

There are volunteers. Tom Crean offers straight away. Vincent puts up his hand, perhaps a little eager to make amends. There's also Marston and McCarthy, buoyed by full bellies and adrenalin and keen to explore the coastline, even though it is far from hospitable.

To the west, Elephant Island looks even less welcoming. Glaciers spill from the interior like thick icing on a cake, and perpendicular cliffs drop straight into churning seas. Dotted high on the rocks are the impossible rookeries of intrepid penguins, where no man in his right mind would consider following, even for a feed. For several hours they sail along the coast, just outside the line of breakers, hoping for something with a bit of promise. When they finally encounter a low gravel spit running at right angles to the coast, their relief is intense.

'That's our spot,' Wild says definitively.

Its suitability is immediately obvious. For one, it's relatively flat. Secondly, it is several metres above the high tide mark. The beach runs out at right angles from the land 100 metres or so to a rocky point. Most importantly, there is a dependable source of water. Up behind the beach, a glacier slope extends down from black peaks. Its rutted surface is a crumbling mess. Judging by the irregular blocks of ice that have been washed up onto the gravel spit, the glacier regularly calves chunks of the bluest ice, perfect for melting.

'Won't be thirsty for a very long time,' says McCarthy.

It is after eight in the evening when they return with good tidings. Tents have been pitched, the other boats pulled clear of the breakwater. The glow of the blubber stove lights their way in the dark, thoughtfully set up in the doorway of a tent away from the wind. Most men are asleep and have been for hours, but the Boss finds himself incapable of turning in until Wild and his crew have returned. He is anxious for news.

'How about we call it Cape Wild?' one of the men suggest.

An honour indeed. Wild is pleased beyond measure to have located a suitable spot to make camp; what they chose to call it is secondary. They have been successful and now they can sleep. There's general agreement that Cape Wild has a ring to it, although the men will soon come up with a slight variation on the name which, given the conditions, will seem utterly appropriate: 'Cape Bloody Wild'.

CHAPTER TWENTY

APRIL 1916

No place is perfect. Least of all Cape Wild. The fiendish wind that scours the beach seems to be worse here than anywhere else. It whips up drifts of snow from the steep slopes above their new camp and blasts it down upon the men with fury, forcing it into every crevice and nook in their worn clothing. Anything not tied down is snatched away in gusts and eddies as they hurry to carry stores above the waterline.

A blizzard makes conditions on their first night at Cape Wild as wet and miserably cold as at sea. Sleeping bags haven't had a chance to dry out and squeezing down into sodden reindeer fur is a ghastly new experience. The large eight-man tent is shredded to bits, its fabric so rotten that it doesn't stand a chance in the wind. At dawn on their second day the occupants of the defunct tent are wrapped in the canvas like grim-faced babies.

Against all odds, Green manages to dish up breakfast during the maelstrom. As hotly as Green's morning hoosh is anticipated, it cannot be delivered swiftly enough. The weather guarantees that it is stone cold before it reaches the men's waiting mouths.

'Food's ruined, you miserable beggar, Lees!'

It feels good to blame someone. Orde-Lees is the one who carried it in the handle-less saucepan from the makeshift galley to where the men languish with long faces, already submerged under 5 centimetres of drift.

'How ungrateful some people can be,' Orde-Lees mutters. His own meal has already started to freeze before he's finished doling out breakfast for the others.

Seeking protection from the gale and snow squalls by whatever means possible occupies the entire day. Fine snow infiltrates even the tents that have thus far survived the wind. Some men fare better than others. The Boss encourages the men wrapped in frozen canvas to find refuge in the *Caird*.

It's not a ready shelter. The boat is half-full of snow itself and, in the absence of shovels or buckets, using hands is the only way to empty it out. Ice, several inches thick, must also be scraped and chipped off the floor and thwarts before they can all wriggle in. Two long hours they work, taking turns with the tools, their bare skin fast becoming frost nipped in the short bursts of activity out of mitts.

By the time they stretch a couple of sails and the remains of their tent over the boat, the men are chilled to the core. Happy to shut the world out, they pull the cover over their new home like a blanket over a great wooden cradle. It proves far from cosy. Beads of ice creep in and the wind harasses the cover until there's precious little screening from the blizzard. After the morning's hard labour, they're no better off.

When Shackleton seeks volunteers for a hunting party, they tumble out of their strange abode into driving snow with bitter expressions. Skinning penguins is the only warmth they're likely to get.

The men in the hoop tents fall victim to the fiercest gusts the second night. What's immediately apparent is that shelter is their chief concern. The much-assailed occupants of the *Caird* have decided to build a stone hut between two large rocks. A feeling of great purpose consumes the men all morning and they're pleased with their progress. They're even more pleased when the Boss tells them they can overturn the *Dudley Docker* and use it as the hut's roof. He wants the *Caird* back now; the boat is needed for its original purpose.

For despite having his feet firmly planted on dry land, Shackleton's mind is already back at sea. Time is short. To stay here indefinitely is not an option. If the savage blizzard is an indication of things to come, any length of time at Cape Wild will be barely survivable.

For so long, reaching land was their raison d'être. Although their ultimate goal is to get home, what comes next is sketchy at best. What they do know is: rescue is not imminent. Firstly, nobody knows where they are. Secondly, Elephant Island is not frequented by the whaling fleet. Thirdly, there is a war. Money and manpower are deployed elsewhere. It's a classic case of out of sight, out of mind.

They have five weeks' worth of food. Even if they succeed in supplementing their rations with seal and penguin meat, some brave soul will need to venture forth for help. Otherwise they will die of starvation. At a little over 800 kilometres away to the north, the Falkland Islands remain the closest inhabited land. Unfortunately, prevailing winds from the north-west would make it virtually impossible to sail there in their fragile boat. South Georgia, despite being much further away – some 1200 kilometres across thunderous seas – is far more favourably located to the east. If they could reach it, a whaling vessel could be chartered to return for the stranded men.

Contemplating such a voyage is exhausting, particularly given their recent terrifying ordeal in the relatively sheltered fringe of the Weddell Sea; what the Boss is proposing is to sail across the worst ocean in the world.

If one man is up to the challenge, it is Frank Worsley. He volunteers immediately. Wild offers too; and Tom Crean. All three are ideal companions for such a risky voyage, but can Shackleton justify taking his top men? It is not just the prospects of the ocean-going men that he needs to consider – the survival of the castaways on Elephant Island is also at stake. Splitting into two groups will require him to appoint a new leader to take over in his absence.

Despite his uncertainty around choice of crew, Shackleton has no doubts regarding the most suitable vessel. The *James Caird* is the only boat up to the task of travelling such a vast distance. Looking over the boat with Worsley and Chippy, he can see that further adjustments will be needed to make her ready for mountainous seas. The *Dudley Docker* can be cannibalised for timber. The mast from the *Stancomb Wills* could be used to reinforce the keel. Chippy suggests they use the lids and nails from provision boxes to close in her front section. While not waterproof, tent canvas pulled taut across the decking would do an adequate job of repelling water. It's nobody's idea of an ideal situation, but it will have to do.

'You'd better come, Chippy,' says Shackleton. 'There'll be plenty of ice about. We might need a carpenter to repair damage to the hull.'

Chippy doesn't bat an eyelid when he's offered the chance to escape aboard the *James Caird*. 'Of course I'll come,' he huffs. 'I don't think there will be many survivors if they have to put in a winter here.'

Accurate navigation is just as critical to their success as a sound vessel. Worsley must come too. The skipper had the great foresight to calculate distances to all the relevant land masses relative to each other before the *Endurance* sank. He's kept a complete log, recording their position with great accuracy even when they were bouncing about on lumpy seas. Setting a course and maintaining it all the way to South Georgia in a 7-metre lifeboat with just three improvised sails will be a feat requiring stamina, concentration and grit. Worsley has all three in abundance. Besides, he finds the challenge of what lies ahead exhilarating, a true test of his mettle. All his life, he's dreamed of embarking on an odyssey, a great sea adventure where his skills and experience will be pitted against nature's cruellest forces.

Crean is a hardy and dependable Irishman through and through. Shackleton would like him to stay. Wild could use his steadying influence, but Crean is desperate to take to the sea and fairly begs the Boss to take him. In the end Shackleton agrees. Another Irishman, the sailor McCarthy, is also selected. Despite the inconceivable hardships of the past year, McCarthy has managed to maintain his cheerful demeanour. Like Worsley, he is eager to put his seamanship to the test in the Southern Ocean. Vincent too will lend considerable sailing experience. He hasn't endeared himself to the Boss, far from it. He's shown himself to be disruptive and untrustworthy, but Shackleton needs the first-class seaman.

'I need you to stay here, Frank,' Shackleton says with regret.

Wild is crestfallen. No one can rival Wild's experience. He's sailed with Captain Scott, sledged with Mawson, and very nearly conquered the pole with Shackleton. Undertaking a sea journey of such epic proportions would be yet another feather in his cap and an alluring challenge for a man who has dedicated his life to daring deeds. However, the leadership of the men on Elephant Island is arguably of greater importance. It certainly represents a test of endurance. Realistically, no other person is better qualified for the task. It will take a certain kind of man to keep everyone's spirits up and, crucially, conflicts to a minimum. Wild's common sense and agreeableness are a winning combination.

'Give us six months, Frank. If we don't get back, take the lads and try with the other two boats to reach Deception Island. You'll be on the whaling route at least. Whereas us . . . if we're not back by November, you can safely assume that we are lost.'

CHAPTER TWENTY-ONE

APRIL 1916

Captain Worsley writes the date in his logbook – *24 April 1916*. It is a day of great promise for everyone, and a certain amount of anxiety. The skipper feels fortunate to be one of the six men setting out into the unknown. Far harder to be among those left at Elephant Island – bored, powerless to determine their fate and facing weeks, if not months, of uncertainty.

Worsley is in his element: wind, waves, a capable boat, a willing crew. The course he's set will take them through the Screaming Sixties, where the world's most severe westerly winds rip around the planet unhindered by land. There should be nothing daunting about it for a sailor with the necessary tools: a sextant, a compass, a couple of chronometers, good charts and navigational tables. It helps that he also has a lifetime of experience.

The *Caird* is handling better with fewer bodies on board and less cargo than last time. In fact, they have had to use shingle and a few larger stones to weigh her down. Ballast of more than a tonne was shovelled into bags sewn from blankets and loaded around the keel. A little too much perhaps, but Shackleton insisted, and the captain had no interest in getting into a scrap on the eve of their departure.

To be fair, the boat leaves a lot to be desired. Even with considerable improvements, the *Caird* is ill-equipped to venture forth on a journey such as theirs. It feels a touch flimsy and it is too small even for six men. As it is, they need to plan all their movements carefully. Every action requires an opposite to avoid capsizing. Three men will take watch while three men will rest under the new decking in the front section. Four hours on, four hours off will be their routine. Steering, watching the sails, bailing – the list of jobs is simple. Preparing meals will be an interesting exercise. A month's worth of food has been loaded, along with two 140-litre water containers and some blocks of glacier ice for extra drinking water. They don't have a galley as such.

Cooking and eating will be a balancing act and require elaborate choreography, all while being hounded by the elements.

On their first night, Worsley and Crean position themselves opposite each other, foot to foot with their backs wedged against the hull. This human frame appears steady enough to hold the Primus stove. Crean is quick to light the flame while Worsley's hands hover near the pot, poised to grab it when the boat lurches. Ice is added in small chunks and once it reaches temperature, pemmican ration is stirred in. Fuel is as precious as food. Not a moment is wasted. Once the meal is heated through, the flame is extinguished.

Spoons and dishes are at the ready. The lack of headroom is a problem. The men must eat doubled over, which makes swallowing difficult, especially when they must eat so quickly. Hot and slick, supper disappears down the throat, scalding the tongue and the stomach. The first one to finish swaps places with the man who's steering. He'll need his fill too. The warmth spreading throughout their bodies is short-lived. Once it hits the fingers and toes, it has already faded from the core.

Vincent keeps his mouth shut and his eye on the sails while Chippy stares out on the waves with grim focus. Crean hums a dirge. McCarthy has a ready smile.

'Fine day for it,' he says the following morning. And it is

a fine day – their first day – as they tend north. But it doesn't stay that way.

'Don't know where this northerly gale came from,' says Crean, holding the steering lines. 'It'll drive us back down south into the pack ice if we're not careful.'

'That would be a death sentence,' says Worsley darkly. 'For us, and those poor Elephant Islanders.'

The boat lurches on, fighting the wind, clashing with the waves, which seem in active disagreement with each other. The confused state of the swell is disagreeable in the extreme for the men; not so for the penguins that leap and dive alongside the boat. Nausea starts to grab. Even Vincent, who has not experienced seasickness in decades, finds his stomach turning inside out. Only Worsley and McCarthy hold their last meal.

After heaving repeatedly over the side of the boat, the Boss turns to Worsley and says grimly, 'Skipper, if anything happens to me while those fellows are waiting for rescue, I shall feel like a murderer.'

The comment strikes a sombre note, which is quite out of step with Shackleton's usual buoyant attitude. It's hard to quote poetry when feeling so wretched. The simple truth in his statement resonates with all of them. It is not just the Boss who feels the weight of responsibility. The successful outcome of this mad enterprise will affect many lives. Not just those of their comrades, with whom they have under-gone such trials, but whole families back in England, whose fervent prayers for the safe return of their missing men have thus far gone unanswered.

Thoughts of his own wife and children back in London are a luxury. Sometimes Shackleton allows himself to drift to them before sleep. Tender details he calls to mind, the sound of a voice, the touch of a hand. Not at present though. Currently his mind is too crowded with the Elephant Islanders to devote much mental energy to his own cherished kin, whose needs are not so great.

CHAPTER TWENTY-TWO

MAY 1916

A decent, deep sleep, one that repairs frayed nerves and freshens the outlook, is what they need most at the end of their first week at sea. But it is simply not possible on the *James Caird*. Nodding off is not such a problem; they've all dozed off inadvertently while sitting at the tiller, even closed their eyes mid-meal, which is surprising given their great enthusiasm for food. It seems cruel then, that as soon as an exhausted man finishes his watch and crawls below the deck, longing for sweet surrender, all of creation conspires to deprive him of that one thing he desires so intently: sleep.

A body at rest is at the mercy of the waves. No matter how well wedged between boxes and bulwarks, the unlucky man still slides up and down, hurled fore-and-aft, frequently banging his head on the underside of the leaking deck whenever rogue waves send a jolt through the hull. Perhaps the freezing sea water leaking onto his face will be the thing to wake him after only seconds of rest. Maybe a nightmare prompted by the suffocating odour of their rotting reindeer sleeping bags will rouse him. If, by some miracle, those things do not bother him and he drifts off to sleep, he need only wait a few minutes before one of the ballast stones will roll into his knees or ricochet off his poor aching back.

Lack of sleep, poor food, the cold, the wind and the horror of being soaked to the skin day-in day-out, as well as the preceding months of hardship, have taken an enormous toll. Vincent is flagging. Inflammation in his limbs caused by sitting for such long periods is not helped by his feet and lower legs being constantly wet. The sailor is not yet a lost cause. That may come. The Boss, ever watchful, is quick to spot a man at a low ebb. Ready to suggest a hot drink, he can often turn things around, provoke a weary smile. But Vincent is past smiling or even speaking.

Progress has been solid, a good distance covered in the time, due partly to skill, but mostly to the sub-Antarctic gales speeding their passage east. A mighty swell is easier to ride when the waves are staggered at regular intervals and the roll of breakers can be anticipated, even if they rain down like angry blows to the head. The *Caird* ships a fair amount of water through the cockpit. The canvas that was once pulled taut across the makeshift decking now slumps under pools of sea water and leaks into the hull. It's not poor workmanship on Chippy's part. The nails they salvaged were too short and are slowly working loose. Unsurprisingly, bailing is a full-time occupation.

Slightly more successful is the hastily constructed pump, a parting gift from Hurley, which has enabled them to keep the bilge water to a reasonable level. It's the devil's own job to operate it, with one man pumping furiously and one poor unfortunate working the nozzle, his hands submerged in the icy brine. Five minutes is all anyone can manage. The agony of frostbitten hands can reduce a man to tears. At least while frozen, a man's extremities lack all sensation; when he starts to massage the blood back into shrunken capillaries, it can feel like having one's fingers or toes slammed in a door.

Despite expecting milder temperatures as they edge further north, the men feel the weather is getting steadily worse. The winds have increased in severity and it is bitterly cold. So cold that the sails freeze to rigid boards. The sea responds with its own changes. Winds rake the tops of waves, the chop increases, and the boat becomes even more ungainly. The best course of action seems to be to hove-to, lash the helm, set a sea anchor to keep the boat pointing in the right direction while they all get some desperately needed rest.

The sails will need to be hauled in. Heavy with ice, they could pull the *Caird* right over if laced with more sea spray. After what seems like hours, the six men settle under the decks. Dog tired, they surrender to the roll and lurch, each fleeing into a sleep-state so deep and black that dreams daren't follow. Five hours straight they doze. When they finally wake, it's with the same uneasy feeling that something is very wrong. The deck is no longer leaking and the boat is subject to a strange leaden motion, a new rhythm that none of them can explain.

'Not good, this!' Worsley shouts from the cockpit. He's the first to see how much ice has accumulated on the topside of the *Caird* from all the water freezing on contact. The ice is almost a foot thick in places. His head bobs below deck. 'We're going to capsize if we don't get rid of it.'

Crean ventures forth to assist Worsley but they can't both shimmy along the deck. The bow is too heavy as it is. Worsley grips to the mainmast and attempts what many would consider the impossible. Aiming deftly, he chops a handhold, then a foothold before striking the sheath of ice with greater force, his one free arm at full extension with Chippy's axe swinging wildly with each jerk of the boat. Fair-sized chunks pop off but he can't keep at it as his hands have lost all feeling after only a couple of minutes. Already sea spray is freezing his body to the spot where he lies prone, taking the odd wave full in the face.

He's a shivering mess by the time Crean helps him back through the hatch. Within minutes of taking his place, Crean is seeking refuge from the barrage of wind and sea water. The job takes hours. Taking it in turns, they work in short bursts well into the night. While they're all aware that sliding into the water is the real danger, it comes as a shock when a wave hits the *Caird* broadside and Vincent is flung free of his handhold. Howling with fright, Vincent is found hanging over the water, one arm wrapped around a frozen oar. When Worsley hauls him to safety he launches into a tirade of abuse. The seaman feels aggrieved. He cannot understand that Worsley's fury is purely an emotional release after hours of pent-up fear and adrenalin.

When the work is done, they eat. Never has a hot meal tasted so good. Chippy slurps loudly in appreciation, then gags. He coughs repeatedly as if trying to loosen something that has caught in his throat. His eyes start to water but nobody pays much attention. It's a frequent enough occurrence. He spits out a hairball and mutters an obscenity. Crean's fingers are black with soot and blubber, covered in small cuts and blisters, and ringed with successive frostbites. Nobody objects when he reaches with his filthy hand and scoops out the mat of fur floating in the hoosh pot. They're sick to death of the wiry hairs that cover them head to toe as well as coat every surface, their food and drink. Every day the balding patches on their four communal sleeping bags grow larger. They look positively diseased and are cold, slimy and sour-smelling to wriggle into after finishing the watch. It's preferable to freezing to death, but to bury one's head in the sodden, decaying space is to imagine suffocation inside the belly of a beast.

'If the seas don't kill us, and the cold doesn't get us, these noxious bags will.'

Shackleton heaves two of the worst-smelling bags out from the crawl space. Grunting with the effort of hoisting their inflated weight over the side, he shouts, 'Good riddance!'

CHAPTER TWENTY-THREE

MAY 1916

Worsley can sense the calm presence in the darkness. It's almost midnight, another evening of angry seas with the howling wind harassing them in an endless rush. The albatross will be out there somewhere, soaring ahead of the south-westerly gale in a state of unhurried freedom, not in the least perturbed. It has kept pace with their progress for more than a week. No matter how dire the sea conditions, the seabird maintains the same effortless rhythm, tipping and dipping its elegant wingspan, swooping up the troughs between waves and skimming over the crests, blithely employing the very same forces that the *Caird* has been fighting for almost ten days.

A wave slams against the bow and drenches Worsley, head to toe. He curses the sea's timing. A dousing is a dousing but all the more unpleasant just as one's four-hour watch is ending. He can hear Shackleton cackling; it's always curiously satisfying to laugh at another's misfortune.

'Bit juicy,' Shackleton says as he emerges into the weather to take over. Another wave hits. This time, the Boss collects it full in the face. Worsley laughs this time. The alternative is to cry.

Worsley ducks his head low. And now the delicate dance commences: the slow slithering into place under the decking, the manoeuvring of damp bodies and boxes and wriggling down into hateful wet reindeer fur. It's quite the comedy. So many straightforward acts have been reduced to absurdity on this voyage. Trying to cook, trying to eat, trying to maintain some dignity while going to the toilet. Every attempt to take a sighting with the sextant is like a circus performance. Worsley swings wildly, with one arm wrapped around the mast, or balances on the thwarts with Vincent and McCarthy holding tight to his legs, all the while with the boat bucking like a mule. It's a wonder they're still on course.

Up in the cockpit, Shackleton peers into the darkness. Nothing but waves and sky, but his eyes register a confusing sight and it takes him a moment to figure out what it is. 'Weather's clearing!' he says to Crean and Chippy, who have taken over the tiresome pumping from Vincent and McCarthy.

But the line of white just discernible in the distance is not clouds lifting at all; it is a wave so enormous that it reaches the sky and stretches the full breadth of the horizon. As it approaches, it looms ever larger until it seems to sit right on top of them. Shackleton stares at it uncomprehending for several seconds. What follows seems to happen in slow motion. Crean lifts his head from the cockpit. Chippy too watches in disbelief as a veritable wall of black water rises before them. In silence the *Caird* rises, rises until the boat is almost perpendicular. When it breaches, it is flung forward like a dart.

'For God's sake, hold on!' Shackleton yells.

The force is such that Shackleton topples backwards. His cries are lost as the *Caird* is catapulted into the wave's violent backwash. The entire sea seems to pass above their heads in an avalanche of sound and spray as thick as smoke. There are crashes and muffled shouts from below deck.

Shackleton can feel a body beneath him but he can't move yet because everything is still in motion. It takes a moment for him to realise that his eyes are shut. When he opens them, he sees water tumbling into the hull, through the cracks, over the sides. His mouth tastes of salt and blood but incredibly, he still holds the steering lines. And the men? It's a miracle none of them have been washed away. They all scramble to the most obvious task, grabbing what they can to empty the water that sits knee-deep in the bottom of the boat. For five frantic minutes they bail. They don't want to disappear without a trace. Not after all this.

Finally the *Caird* recovers its equilibrium. The Boss steadies the sails and they resume their course as if the whole episode was just a peculiar dream. The albatross sweeps overhead, showing only mild curiosity about the recent drama. The remaining distance to South Georgia means nothing to him. He'd be there in a day at most.

CHAPTER TWENTY-FOUR

MAY 1916

'Land ho!' McCarthy shouts.

Wind-scarred and weary, the men gaze on the fine, solid thing to the north-east. With every hour it grows larger, blacker, imposing itself on the horizon, a statement of fact. To plant one's feet on something firm, to walk upright will feel unimaginably good after two weeks of sitting hunched at the tiller, scrambling about the cockpit, and slithering on their bellies in stinking dark spaces. Worsley has achieved the virtually impossible. His navigation has proved faultless despite his numerous challenges. Against all odds, he has got them here. They have done it!

South Georgia looks unfamiliar from this side of the island. Grytviken, where they spent a month with the Norwegians, is on the opposite coast, along with every other whaling station or habitation. Sailing around the coast to one of these outposts will be their next challenge. A couple of hundred kilometres more. So close; so much further to go. Still, they cannot wipe the smiles off their faces.

After their last 38-litre cask of drinking water was found to be tainted with the brackish water that sloshes constantly about their feet, they have suffered the most excruciating thirst. For several days now their salty mouthfuls have been close to undrinkable. Salvation could not come soon enough. Vincent sips at a small cupful with cracked lips, silent and sullen. He won't last. Physically he's broken; his mental state is shaky. Chippy is in a bad way too. He says that he's spent and cannot go any further. Good thing the boat is bearing them along; if they had to carry their own weight, the end would have come several days ago.

Making landfall is their primary aim. The need for rest and water is dire. Only a few kilometres offshore and with a tremendous westerly wind picking up, keeping a level head is paramount. It's late afternoon; they'll soon be losing the light and the ability to choose a safe landing site. This is no time for undue risk or rash decisions. Reefs and rocks are

Worsley's nightmare at the best of times but in uncharted waters such as these, high winds and rough seas pose even more of a hazard to navigation. They might be blown onto cliffs and smashed to smithereens. Drowning is the worst they can expect, but a beach landing in a fierce swell could also put their plan into jeopardy. Sustaining any kind of injury, whether a broken limb or fractured skull, in such an isolated location would be disastrous. Once again, their thoughts fly back to their castaway comrades. Avoiding catastrophe is all that matters.

'Dirty weather's coming,' says Worsley. 'Dare we make a run for King Haakon Sound?'

'Not with this westerly blowing. We'll be driven onto the rocks.' Shackleton pauses. The next part is hard for him to say. 'We'll need to come about. Head out to sea again.'

They're all in agreement. The rumble of surf pounding the shore makes any attempt to land a prospect more terrifying than another night in the *Caird*, even if tortured by thirst, even if battling a storm. It takes McCarthy and Crean fifteen minutes to wrestle down the mainsail and mizzen, to get them reefed. The ballast stones are shifted to steady the boat against the storm surge.

Bent low under the decking, Vincent and Chippy find it backbreaking work. They're still at it when the weather hits with a sudden intensity that is deafening. The twisting confusion of rain and hailstones seems to last hours. As the wind builds, so does the swell. Each successive wave that ploughs into them threatens to swamp the boat and drag them down. Worsley wedges himself at the tiller, while the other men focus on ridding the *Caird* of water; Shackleton, Crean and McCarthy at the pump, and Chippy and Vincent frantically working by hand.

The hurricane's bombardment lasts all night and drags the men exhausted through the following day. Straining the dregs of liquid from their water cask through gauze from the medical kit, they manage to collect the grit and hair; it doesn't do a thing for the taste. Brackish residue scarcely seems worth the effort. How they would love to turn their backs on the deep, to be finally free of its brininess. Salt water seems to run in their veins. Even the rain tastes of it.

So little remains of their resolve as they face a second night at sea within sight of the island but unable to land. Worsley thinks of his precious log. The pains he has taken to keep a record throughout their ordeal. He cannot bear the idea of it sinking to the bottom of the sea, for their heroic story to remain untold. Crean would love nothing more than to light his pipe and take a deep drag of smoke into his lungs. Shackleton just thinks of his men and works the pump with renewed vigour.

When the new day dawns, the wind drops. The odd petulant wave slamming into the *Caird* is all that remains of the storm's rage. How swiftly fortunes change! Crawling from below to see the sky clearing, Tom Crean knocks the pin securing the *Caird*'s mast. Worsley sees it topple but McCarthy is the one who grabs it as it crashes into the sea. Together they wrangle it back into position while Crean steadies the operation from below and rams the pin into place. Only then does he examine the nasty gouge where it tore into his side.

'Must have worked loose in the storm,' observes McCarthy.

Shackleton can't believe it. 'If it had popped out then, we'd have lost the mast. We'd have been finished.'

They cling to this one piece of luck as the wind changes to offshore. Once again, their poor boat is shunted out to sea. Down come the sails and the oars are slotted into the rowlocks. Manpower is what's required. At least they feel more in control of their fate, not so passive. Despite it being a bitter fight that they seem scarcely capable of winning, they row like never before. For hours they pull against the tide and the wind, against months of deprivation, against their own desire to finally admit defeat.

'It's been five hundred and twenty-two days since we left South Georgia,' says Worsley.

'And it shan't be one day longer,' says the Boss.

It has taken sixteen days to reach these shores. Slopes of green tussock dotted with nesting albatrosses greet the travellers but beyond that, the imposing sight of snowy mountains, hundreds of metres high, is a brutal reminder of another impossible challenge awaiting them. They scan the rock-lined bays of King Haakon Sound all afternoon. When a cove presents itself, it seems to be the only safe landing spot in a hostile land. The scrape of the hull sliding to a stop on shingle is the sweetest sound any of them could imagine. They tumble from the *Caird* and, on unsteady legs, make for the narrow stream meandering across the boulder-strewn beach. Dropping to their hands and knees, they plunge their faces into the fresh water and drink.

PART IV

ENDURANCE

CHAPTER TWENTY-FIVE

MAY 1916

Chippy McNish appreciates an opportunity to be on his own. In the long grass, sitting on this hillside looking down at the sea puts him in mind of home. Ever closer. The cove is but a temporary place to stay but it's been good to rest up for a few days and recuperate. The cave further up the beach offers adequate shelter, especially with sails stretched across the entrance. Worsley has made it even more comfortable with armfuls of tussock laid out on the rocky ground.

There's a sudden rushing sound as an albatross swoops over Chippy's head to land further up the hillside.

So graceful in the air, so ungainly on their feet, the albatrosses cannot make a speedy getaway when pursued. With
wings that are too long to manoeuvre quickly among the
scrubby growth and a lumbering gait, they make the easiest
of targets and a delicious feast. With plentiful fresh water
and a ready food supply, they'll want for nothing while they
regain their strength.

Several days of sleeping stretched out by a fire has been
luxury after more than two weeks at sea. Their clothes are
dry for the first time in months. And to have room to move!
If he wanted to, Chippy could fling his arms about and for
once not risk hitting anyone in the face. But he's still too
depleted of energy for acrobatics.

Vincent is in a worse state, covered in saltwater sores,
his legs numb and swollen like the limbs of a corpse. He lies
in the sleeping bag, stoking the fire with the top sections of
the *Caird*. He had made a show of unloading the boat but
then collapsed in a heap. He couldn't even rouse himself
when Crean was dragged off his feet in the turning tide and
the rest of them had to scramble to save the *Caird*. Thankfully they hadn't lost Crean or the boat, but they had lost
the rudder. Their trusty boat is unlikely to make another
sea journey of any great distance. Certainly, a voyage around
South Georgia to the opposite coast appears an imposs-
ibility. What seems more likely now is a trek through the
interior.

The plan is discussed that night as they warm themselves by the fire. The following day they will sail further up the inlet to the very end of King Haakon Sound. This will give them a clear run at the mountains. Nobody has crossed them before – or even mapped the interior of South Georgia. Worsley and Crean, the most physically able, will accompany the Boss who, as always, is confident of a successful outcome.

Of course, there will be more ghastly, changeable weather, snow and ice. None of that is new. But mountaineering is. Without any equipment save a length of alpine rope and totally unsuitable footwear, it's an unsettling thought. Suppressing any private misgivings, the men focus on warmth and companionship and lively conversation.

'The first time I clocked one, I felt like a murderer,' says Worsley, handing Crean one of the skinned albatross chicks to roast over the fire. 'Those big eyes, powder puff bodies.'

'And then you tasted it,' says Crean with a grin.

'Oh yes!'

'Even the bones taste good,' adds McCarthy.

'Imagine the price these would fetch in London or New York,' says Worsley with enthusiasm. 'There'd be no shortage of wealthy men prepared to pay a fortune for this. The rare delight of South Georgian albatross chicks! I reckon we could sell them for fifty pounds a pop. Wouldn't be a bad way to fund your next expedition, Boss.'

'Pity there are regulations against it,' says Shackleton.

'Oops,' says Crean.

Chippy says, 'Well, with all the chicks we've consumed in the last four days, we're already running foul of the law.'

Worsley shrugs. 'Not the law of necessity.'

'I hope we find a good supply where we're going,' says Crean.

'Where we're going, is home,' says Shackleton emphatically. 'You can eat whatever you like there.'

'Though maybe not albatross chicks,' says Worsley archly.

CHAPTER TWENTY-SIX

MAY 1916

It's mid-May. Nine days since they arrived in South Georgia. Shackleton is impatient. They must get going. His mood has darkened. Dismal weather hasn't helped. A fine spell is what they need for the crossing. And a full moon. Days are short. They'll be climbing well into the night. His anxiety rises with each passing day. The Boss pictures his men 1300 kilometres away on Elephant Island. Almost a month has passed since their farewell.

Shackleton hands the diary back to Chippy. It's in writing now – his final orders. Chippy is to be left in charge of McCarthy and Vincent. The upturned *Caird* will be their home at the tip of King Haakon Sound. The beach always has seals basking nearby. That will be good for food. But with a limited number of cartridges for the shotgun, they won't be able to survive indefinitely. The Boss has written down the general plan: how he, Crean and Worsley will make for the whaling settlement of Stromness on the other side of South Georgia. The decision to leave three members of his team is not taken lightly – he realises he might need to answer to charges of abandoning his men. He needs to make his orders clear.

'Do you understand?'

The carpenter reads the words again: *In the event of my non-return you had better, after winter is over, try and sail round to the East Coast.*

Chippy sighs. '"In the event of your *non-return*"? What do you mean by that? Do you think you might not get back for us for a while?' Chippy is working up a head of steam. 'You know we won't last winter here on this exposed beach.'

'I mean death.'

Chippy is silent for a few seconds. 'How long will it take?'

'A few days,' says Shackleton. Really, he has no idea.

After months of heavy use, their clothing is threadbare, rotting away in places. It offers little protection from wind and none from the cold. They have holey socks, unravelling jerseys, and balaclavas in need of repair. A knapsack would be a fine thing to carry all their items – matches, two compasses, a Primus and some fuel, binoculars and food for three days packed into socks – but everything hangs off their bodies, tied on with lengths of lamp wick. The alpine rope is the heaviest thing they must carry, but it is extremely handy. Chippy's axe will also prove indispensable. The carpenter has fitted brass screws to the soles of the men's boots. Simple crampons that they all hope will last the distance. He's also made them each a walking stick from lengths of driftwood. Chippy's last parting gift must be the most generous, but the Boss refuses it.

'That's kind of you. But I don't want the extra weight.'

Chippy nods. The sleeping bags are horrendously heavy.

'But you don't have a tent,' says McCarthy.

'We're not going to stop,' says Shackleton. 'Sleep is a luxury we cannot afford.'

Their final night together is far from restful. Shackleton is up checking the weather every few hours. It's looking promising when Worsley joins him, full of nervous tension. The two men agree that they must set out at once. They rouse Crean and after a hastily consumed breakfast, strike out. The moon is bright at 3 a.m. and the way is clear. Chippy and McCarthy accompany them for a stretch before wishing them well and turning for home.

The early sections of the route are familiar. They've walked up to the saddle several times, but they have no idea what lies beyond that point. Despite the slippery surface, they make good progress on the upward march, stopping every fifteen minutes for a breather. They seem to be hitting their stride when a thick fog briefly separates them from their surroundings. Deprived of outside stimulus, their footfalls become their sole focus. There is something pleasing about their feet maintaining an even rhythm in the snow.

'Skipper!' Shackleton calls sharply. 'Stop!'

Worsley is brought up short. 'What the heck . . . ?'

Further back, Crean curses softly as he sees the crevasse. The fall would have been deadly. Just looking at the gaping hole before them sets his heart racing. They've been much too cavalier.

'Won't be the last,' Shackleton says. 'Better rope up.'

Worsley lifts the 15 metres of alpine rope from his aching shoulders. It lands on the snow with a heavy thud. With his hands freed up, it will be a lot easier to read the compass.

The view from the saddle is splendid in the moonlight. To see so far and wide, to be so high above everything is thrilling after months of grubbing about at sea level. In the silvery glow the landscape has a crispness to it that is offset by banks of billowing mist that extend to the horizon. Below them is a large white lake. The fact that it's frozen means they can probably walk across it to save time. At first the downhill approach across a snowfield appears none too taxing, but what soon becomes apparent is that they are walking on a glacier. Despite being roped for safety, they are still anxious. Crevasses are not always visible and falling down one could spell disaster. Stopping to assess their route, the men snatch a bite of cold pemmican. Not the tastiest snack, but with a biscuit and a couple of lumps of sugar, it delivers some well-needed energy. A handful of snow is the closest they get to a drink; there's no point setting up the Primus this early on in their march. They need to keep on. Dawn is breaking.

'Sorry, but that's no lake,' says Crean, pointing ahead. 'We're looking at the sea.'

'You're joking,' says Worsley with dismay.

'He's not,' says the Boss. 'That's Possession Bay. We've been heading north, not east.'

'We're going to have to retrace our steps, aren't we? Back up the hill.'

None of them like to admit to the intense feelings of frustration. So much wasted effort. This early on, it's gutting. Without an accurate map, it won't be the only time they get it wrong.

Once the sun's slanting rays are upon them, they begin to feel better. Even more so when they realise they can skirt around the slope rather than head directly up. Worsley's morale has improved markedly. He even finds himself looking around appreciatively at the alpine scenery bathed in early morning light. Nobody talks. The only sound is the crunch of snow and the odd deep breath as they ascend towards a dramatic formation of craggy pinnacles that look like extended fingers. Beyond, to the south-east, the Allardyce Range forms an uneven spine of mountains that would take them all the way to Grytviken if they could step magically from mountain-top to mountain-top. Stromness is closer, thankfully, and if they keep going in a straight line, they shouldn't need to scale the sheer-sided mountains to get there.

Keeping to a straight line proves far from pleasant. Breaking a trail in knee-deep snow is a tiring way to pass the morning. Every fifteen minutes they fall on their backs and gulp in lungfuls of air while trying not to think of the continuing exertion ahead. Another three hours of hard slog and they stop for lunch. Worsley and Crean shield the Primus with their bodies while the little stove pumps out enough heat to melt some snow for a pemmican hoosh. They don't bother with plates. They each have a spoon and once their modest meal is warmed through, they dive into the common pot without delay. They are ravenously hungry but happy to be together and making progress.

'Crean, your spoon is bigger than ours,' says Shackleton with mock horror.

'Doesn't matter,' says Crean. 'The skipper has a bigger mouth.'

CHAPTER TWENTY-SEVEN

MAY 1916

Worsley's feet have lost all sensation. After massaging feeling back into his bare toes and heels, he swaps his socks. His boots are dreadfully unsuited to mountaineering, but he has found that if he tightens the laces, he can keep the snow out.

Shackleton looks on with a mix of incredulity and admiration. He's impressed that Worsley has thought to bring spare socks. He considers the insubstantial leather boots on his own feet. They would not look out of place on the streets of London. His snow boots would be far better suited to ice work but they're on another man's feet now. The Boss can't remember who he gave them to – clearly somebody who needed them more than he did.

Pausing for a break was sensible. They need to gather their thoughts. After more than twelve hours on the move, they have yet to find a way over the high pass. From below, the pinnacles that looked to them like extended fingers offered several possible routes. The most direct route ends in a precipice. Doubling back, they focus their efforts on reaching another gap, only to find themselves peering over ice cliffs into nothingness. Even with the best boots, the best equipment in the world, they cannot progress this way. An entire day has been spent trying to negotiate a way forward. A mere 10 kilometres they've travelled. Maybe this is where they admit defeat.

The cold has a penetrating intensity even without the cutting wind whipping up from the valley below. They are at altitude – already at 1200 metres. It makes them feel giddy and spent.

'We could try to get down this way,' Worsley says. 'I've had it with all this backtracking.'

The Boss shakes his head.

Crean simply turns away. What Worsley is suggesting is madness – out of the question.

Their zigzagging search for a way through continues. Down again, up again. The approach to the fourth gap is so steep the Boss must cut steps into the snow. Finally at the top, they hang their heads over the razorback ridge and consider the swoop of the disappearing slope on the other side. Losing the light, they have very few options. Even retreat seems impossible, with an impenetrable bank of fog rolling up the way they came, swallowing every trace of their footsteps.

Crean sits down on the ridge, his legs dangling, as if contemplating a jump into the void. 'I really thought there would be a way through here.'

'Maybe it flattens out further down.' Worsley strains his eyes. 'It's too dim to make anything out now.'

It comes as a surprise when Shackleton says, 'Let's try it.'

With the other two holding the rope taut, Shackleton scrambles over the lip and begins to slash wedges into the hard snow with Chippy's axe. The steps are rough but effective footholds. There are five or six by the time the other two men have eased themselves over the ridge, suddenly as committed to the descent as the Boss. But it's painfully slow going, even as the gradient eases. The cold and darkness press in around them. Each man begins to think exposure or exhaustion will overtake them before they make meaningful headway down the slope.

'Let's just slide.' Shackleton's suggestion is no joke.

'There'll be no stopping once we get up speed,' says Crean.

'No telling what lies ahead either,' warns Worsley.

'A sheer drop? Rocks?'

'Disaster.'

'Well, it will be the death of us if we stay here any longer.'

Agreement is reached. Even if they're killed, at least they will have done everything in their power to save their companions. They untie the rope from their waists and coil it like a mat. The friction will slow their acceleration, though not nearly enough. Worsley fixes his arms and legs around the Boss, Crean does the same to Worsley. The trio are locked together in terrible anticipation.

There's no countdown. Shackleton kicks their make-shift toboggan into motion and they plummet headlong into the mists. They gather more and more speed until they are totally out of control, virtually in freefall, bouncing violently off the surface, their hearts racing and their faces set in expressions of complete terror as if experiencing life's final moments. Snow and ice fly up in a white blur around them and they brace for the inevitable impact. But when the slope starts to ease off, their screams of alarm turn to whoops of exhilaration. Finally a bank of soft snow ends their joyride. They get to their feet and shake each other by the hand. Nobody has a trace of regret but everyone has a sense of having cheated death.

'What do you reckon that was, a drop of 500 metres? In a couple of minutes.'

'It felt like an age,' says Worsley.

'Let's not make a habit of doing that,' says Shackleton.

Crean grins. 'No chance of that, our trousers wouldn't allow it.'

Worsley twists around to view the state of his best dress pants. The hole is not so well-positioned. Good thing he's travelling with friends.

CHAPTER TWENTY-EIGHT

MAY 1916

The adrenalin rush of their mad descent delivers a much-needed boost. It's approaching seven o'clock but there will be no rest this evening. The moon rising from behind peaks illuminates the wide undulating snow field that spreads out before them. To the left is Antarctic Bay, another deep fjord cutting into the land like the one they mistook for a lake. This time there is no mistaking where they are, although distances are hard to judge, particularly in the strange light. What appears a far-off landscape feature turns out to be merely a rocky mound as they pass close by.

The wind is at their backs and the way seems remarkably tame after the afternoon's trials. They rope up and move off in single file up a long, gentle snow field. To the right are two rocky bluffs that run down to icefalls and a heavily crevassed area. Altering their path slightly, they'll keep further to the left to stay clear of danger.

Breath sweeps away from their mouths in cold waves and gathers as frost in their beards. It's a moment to rejoice when the snow hardens underfoot and they no longer sink to their knees. The pace of their march quickens. Soon they are warm. Their thoughts rove freely through the night but never far enough to forget how exhausted they feel. Every half-hour they stop for two minutes of rest, lying on their backs in the snow, gazing up at the expanse of sky and trying desperately not to surrender to sleep. Perhaps it is their lack of sleep combined with the dreamlike glow of the landscape, but each man has a growing sense that they are not alone. The feeling is so pronounced that when Crean turns in his tracks to address the fourth man, he is startled to see only footprints disturbing the pale realm.

Their midnight meal is consumed with great haste, gobbled up without fear of scalding mouths or throats with near-boiling hoosh. Having reached the crest of the long upward slope, they're pleased to see the descent to the large bay is an easy one. Mere hours separate them from the Stromness Harbour whaling station. It is with generous strides fuelled by food that they set forth, their sense of imminent victory driving them on. They fairly canter down the slope. But as the route becomes lumpy, riddled with fissures, they're brought up short. Once again, they have been caught out by misplaced exuberance.

'We're on a glacier, lads,' says Shackleton suddenly.

Worsley finishes the thought: 'No glaciers in Stromness Bay.'

'Then this isn't Stromness Bay.'

They simply turn and head back up the hill. The confusing coastline, the moonlight, their exhaustion; all of it plays a part in the silly but time-consuming mistake. The upward slope to the south-east is a slow slog, made even more unpleasant by their building frustration with the endlessness of their quest, and with each other. Several times, Worsley steps on the safety rope, which brings Crean and the Boss to a jarring halt.

'Watch it!'

'Sorry!'

On the whole they treat each other with exaggerated courtesy. Irritation lies so close to the surface that they are all terrified of it breaking through. They know that it will be impossible to continue without unity.

With this thought in mind, Crean and Worsley offer repeatedly over the next few hours to take the lead. Breaking a trail is an exhausting task and the Boss has been at it since they set out almost twenty-four hours earlier. He won't allow it even though he is clearly flagging as they tackle the steep section to a gap between what looks like two rugged battlements. Keen to snatch a moment's rest near the top, they perch in a rocky alcove and tip their heads back against the solid facing. Shackleton can feel the leaden dip of shoulders beside him as sleep overtakes his two companions. *Better allow them some rest*, he thinks as he fights to keep his eyes on the moon setting in the western sky. After ten minutes he rouses them with a nudge.

'Wake up, boys,' he says briskly. 'That's half an hour you've had.'

It's coming to six o'clock on their second morning by the time they breach the gap. While Crean starts to prepare the meal, Shackleton and Worsley scout the route. The flush of dawn on the eastern horizon offers a clearer picture of what lies below – a sharpish descent towards another dark arm of the sea, and a great flaring cape of a glacier swooping around from the right to meet it. Beyond that, a transverse ridge, easy enough to cross over, and then Stromness on the other side. Did the Boss imagine the blow of a whistle? He cannot be sure enough to mention it to the others, though he remembers that the whistle is blown a second time at seven.

'What's the time, Crean?' Shackleton asks as they finish off their breakfast.

'Just before seven.'

'Let's see if we can hear the whalers' whistle.'

It's a haunting sound, but one that is followed by spirited cheers and ecstatic handshakes. Nothing else matters. Worsley kicks the empty fuel can clear of the Primus with a triumphant shout. It tumbles down the hill, a spent and useless thing. Its weight around his neck will not be missed.

The temptation is to take chances, so close to civilisation, but the Boss will not be hurried. Danger lies ahead: tricky footing on a steep slope that has been polished to a high shine by wind whipping up from the valley below. It takes forever to inch forward, rope taut, the Boss cleaving footholds into the frozen face with the axe. Such cautiousness is admirable. Chunks of ice bounce and skitter off the sheer surface and fly from view. A falling man would fare much the same, and take his companions down with him.

It is the longest descent yet, from an altitude of at least 800 metres, but nobody suggests they repeat their tobogganing exploit. Humour has no place in such a perilous situation. Presently the ice thins out and the strike of the Boss's heel is enough to break it. Worsley smashes down with his own boots, enlarging the Boss's divots so Crean can position his feet securely enough to take the strain from the rope. If either of the trailblazers starts to fall, Crean should be able to hold them until they get purchase. Luckily he is not tested. He's not as strong as he used to be.

When safely down on the flatlands, they look back up at the diagonal trail dotting back and forth across the face. What an odd sight they must have appeared, three men as small as spiders. It's a relief to be following the glacial moraine down to Fortuna Bay. Penguins and sea elephants are a novel sight on the beach, but they don't slacken their pace to admire the wildlife.

Worsley's easterly bearing carries them inland and up a rise. The terrain is rugged and pitted and the up-and-down effort is tiring beyond belief. When they chance upon a flat section they're delighted. Not for long. Crean disappears up to his waist in frigid water. Why had they not realised they were walking on a frozen lake? Foggy brains make everything more taxing.

It is approaching noon before they eat their final meal. A biscuit, a nut bar and a mouthful of snow do little to brighten Crean's mood or dry out his clothes. A hot meal is what he needs, more than ever as the wind intensifies and they press on, accompanied by the squelching of sodden boots.

CHAPTER TWENTY-NINE

MAY 1916

How they will welcome the stink! The rank odour of the open-air butchery, the floating carcasses, pigs rooting around in the half-rotten piles of entrails that slosh about on the tideline. From the top of the ridge they cannot smell a thing, but they see Stromness Bay, hear the industrial sounds echoing up from the harbour and rejoice in the black smoke issuing from the two whale-catchers returning from the sea.

Worsley yells with all his might and waves his arms in desperation. The others stand silhouetted against the skyline and smile at his useless gesture that is nevertheless entirely understandable. A quick way down lies directly at their feet, a scramble of 500 metres or so. Worsley points it out. But Shackleton is back to his 'Cautious Jack' ways.

'Too steep,' he says. 'Let's arrive in one piece.'

He points them to a more sedate-looking route that will lead them off to the left. It should bring them back around once they lose some height. A nearby stream has eroded a path and will provide some surety. They're thoroughly sick of dead ends. If they follow the water down into the gully, they'll reach the shore, no matter what. It's early afternoon. The thought of uninterrupted sleep is intoxicating. There'll be soap and hot water, a hearty meal, a mug of hot coffee – although all of that may need to wait until they wake.

The Boss's mind bolts ahead of his own needs. He's in organisation mode, stepping through a rescue. Eighteen months have passed since they were in Grytviken aboard the *Endurance*. There were plenty of visits to the other Norwegian whaling stations along the coast during that month of waiting – to Leith and Husvik, Stromness. He hopes to find some familiar faces. Men who know hardship are often generous. He expects offers of help will be forthcoming. It shouldn't be too difficult to get back around to King Haakon Sound for Chippy, Vincent and McCarthy. Deciding on a course of action to rescue the Elephant Islanders some 1300 kilometres away will take a great deal longer.

The three men need to watch their step as the path they've chosen gets progressively steeper and the stream cuts deep into the rock and gravelly ground. Before long, they find themselves in a narrow ravine, where it's easier to clamber down the stream bed itself than take chances on the slippery rock walls. Wet boots all round.

'Beastly,' mutters Worsley, wondering if fate could possibly put any more hardships in their path.

But it does. Their progress is brought up short. The ravine falls away into a precipice; the stream is now a waterfall.

'And my way was too steep?' Worsley's comment doesn't help things much.

Crean peers down with a look of dread, then looks back up the way they've come. Another excruciating climb. He shakes his head. 'Shall we abseil?'

The drop is eight metres, ten at most. Shackleton searches Worsley's careworn face for agreement.

Worsley is in no mood to backtrack. 'I'll go last.'

They take a moment to secure the alpine rope over the bulge of a large rock and ram the loose end into a crevice. It's by no means fail-safe, but with the skipper providing another anchor point, it's the best they can expect. The axe lands at the bottom with a clank. The cooking pot too is dropped over the edge, although goodness knows why they feel they need to carry it the last few kilometres.

Shackleton is first over the lip. Once safely at the bottom, he calls for the others to follow. Crean takes on the challenge with all the skill of a dockyard rigger. Finally, it is Worsley's turn. His heart thumps as he assesses the vertiginous drop over the waterfall. Whether he doubts his companions can catch him or the rope will hold him, Worsley couldn't be quicker if he slid down a greased pole. He's terrifically relieved when it's over.

Crean yanks on the rope. 'See, nothing to worry about, Skipper.'

They all have a go, try shaking the end back and forth, tugging it, even flicking it upwards sharply to dislodge it from the crevice, but nothing works. By whatever mysterious means, the rope holds fast.

Low, snow-covered terrain lies ahead. A rope is unlikely to prove necessary to survival. The cooking pot is surplus to requirements and is jettisoned without a backwards glance; the axe, they take. Habit mostly, but also some strange sense of loyalty to those in King Haakon Sound, who surrendered the tool willingly. Their shuffling gait becomes more pronounced as they approach the settlement across icy flats. The screws in the soles of their boots have worn to nothing. Sliding about on unsteady feet, the men see little comedy in the painful falls they each take. Crean's brief encounter with the axe cuts into his already woebegone clothing and he flings it away in a rage.

Thirty-six hours they've been on the move with barely a moment's rest. The final hundred metres lie before them. It is 20 May 1916. They don't quite know how they achieved the impossible; only that they needed to.

'How do I look?' asks Worsley.

The others stare blankly at the skipper. His face is weathered and filthy, his beard is long and matted. The greasy rags he wears would not look out of place on a scarecrow, but still he attempts to tidy himself. From his pocket he takes three safety pins, which he uses to fix the worst of the holes in his trousers.

'Can I have one?' asks the Boss.

'Not on your life,' says Worsley in irritation. 'There might be ladies about.'

In the event, two young lads are the first humans to lay eyes on them. They take one look at the three barbarians staggering out from the interior of the island and turn tail; hardly the welcoming committee they would have liked.

The station manager is called Thoralf Sørlle. Shackleton has met him before. It feels like a lifetime ago. He's a fat, busy fellow, who doesn't suffer fools. When it comes to business, he is a man of few words, and none of them particularly courteous.

'Well?' Sørlle says, when the three shambling figures appear at the door to his office.

'Don't you know me?' asks the Boss.

Sørlle narrows his eyes thoughtfully. 'Your voice, perhaps.'

'My name is Shackleton.'

Sørlle looks like he might faint. 'Lord Almighty, you had better come in.'

Shackleton turns to his two companions and suddenly sees the repugnant state of them. He knows he looks much the same himself. Hardly human. 'I'm afraid we stink.'

Sørlle laughs. 'You do stink! To high heaven. But this is a whaling station. We all stink!'

CHAPTER THIRTY

MAY 1916

Jimmy paces up and down the rough ribbon of beach at Cape Wild, displaying not so much the behaviour of a caged animal as a scientist. He is keen to record the details of their environment in his diary. Scientific precision is not possible; he doesn't even have a measuring tape. In the absence of appropriate instrumentation, he uses his 'eye-chrometer' and the length of his stride. He's figured out the length and height of most of the landscape features – the rocky eminence they call the Point, the narrow channel, the lofty island rock, about 9 metres high, sheer on its landward face.

Understanding the topography of his surroundings brings him fresh joy – there is so much to describe. He'll never tire of the way the knife-edge peaks at the western end of the bay sweep down to the sea in a beautiful hyperbolic curve. Jimmy's eyes sweep up to admire the glacier that tumbles down to the beach. It's astonishing how its colours change from blue to vibrant green to purple and pink as the daylight conditions change. Such wonder to behold even through broken glasses.

Jimmy never wants to go to sea again, but he is even more grateful to be off the ice. Their sixteen-month confinement had been hellish. Even though he attempted to use the time productively, making a rudimentary study of ice formations, he felt his brain starting to fog, to atrophy. Compared to Cambridge, the monotonous vistas and dull company of the ice floe felt like a type of prison, where even geometry studies from the *Encyclopaedia Britannica* failed to hold much allure. He was thankful at least to have Hurley. His friend always had something interesting to say.

The photographer has come to join Jimmy. Together they point out landscape features, speculate about what equipment would be needed to attempt to get onto the glacier and follow the slope all the way up into the interior of the island. The photographer's eye is similarly stimulated. He's taken a few photos since they arrived on Elephant Island but he needs to ration his rolls of film. His relief at having protected his photographic plates during their rough transit by sea is enormous. Survival is but one thing to consider; the potential to turn this whole experience into financial gain is considerable.

In any case, Hurley doesn't consider their situation too perilous. Food supply is not an issue. Gentoo penguins and seals seem as happy to land at Cape Wild as they were. While they would all love a bit of variation in their diet, they're not starving. Green is constantly frying up meat on his makeshift stove. They now have spoonfuls of pungent fat and rendered blubber scratchings at every meal. Of course, Orde-Lees harps on at length about the need to stockpile supplies in case they all disappear, but nobody listens. Such is the contentment of men with full bellies. Who has an appetite for planning ahead when immediate needs are so well met?

Frank Wild says rescue is imminent. Ten days to two weeks was the Boss's estimation of the boat journey to South Georgia. Already they have been gone a month. A mast has been fashioned into a flagpole with a signal flag, ready to hoist at a moment's notice. Until that happy day, routine will prevail. Never does it enter Wild's mind that something bad could happen to Shackleton before he gets to South Georgia. The Boss will return for them. And they should be ready.

Not everyone is as optimistic as Wild. To be once again waiting, waiting, waiting has the effect of bringing pessimists to the fore. Especially when most of the tobacco supply has been smoked to extinction. Wordie is the only man with allocation remaining, a natural consequence of his own careful rationing. Nasty comments are muttered; some suggest that Wordie received more than his fair share. Others put their frustration to better use, experimenting with smoking the sennegrass lining from their finnesko boots or seaweed that has been boiled up in a pot. Coughing fits are generally the result. That and sour expressions.

Each man has his peculiar ways, his shortcomings and irritating habits. There is no hiding them now that they are all jammed into the same cramped lodgings. The Cape Wild hut is an unpretentious abode, ingenious in its construction. It is the product of constant improvements made by all twenty-two men who call it home. The interior is dark and dank. It smells of belching, farting, humid bodies that have not seen soap or had a change of underclothes in almost a year. Thankfully nobody smells worse than his neighbour and so responsibility for the general stench is not pinned on any one person. Then there's the blubber stove for heating the hut. The greasy odour emanating from it at all times of the day does an admirable job of covering the more offensive smells that do occasionally invade the space.

During the sea crossing the men had come to detest every inch of chipped paintwork of the small lifeboats; afterwards they felt seasick at the mere sight of them. The

Stancomb Wills and the *Dudley Docker* have redeemed themselves. They make a far better shelter than they did lifeboats. Upturned on a low wall of rocks, they are quite fit for purpose, a match for any southerly gale.

Frank Wild's strict routine keeps matters orderly and straightforward. It starts with each occupant having his assigned sleeping spot. There's insufficient room on the ground floor, so several men roost on the thwarts above the others. Once everybody is inside, Marston can sling his hammock against the entrance. The stove is kept smouldering with blubber day and night. Those whose sleeping spot is squeezed alongside it are not always comforted by the warmth. At times, the heat is oppressive. Despite this, it is probably considered the most privileged position in the hut.

Orde-Lees certainly uses it to his advantage. He has quite the collection of little tins in which he conducts his own cooking operations in miniature using the scraps of food he saves from almost every meal. The others view his hoardings of odds and ends as further evidence of his miserly nature. A quarter of a nut bar here, a nibbled rind of seal meat there; they're all tasty snacks. Sometimes the other men's jibes and taunts are rather cruel, but Orde-Lees's manner is so irritating that even the two doctors fantasise about strangling him.

Wild tries in vain to keep his anger in check. On occasion he has shouted so loudly at Orde-Lees that he strained his vocal cords. It is Orde-Lees's priggishness, his eccentricity, his thunderous snoring that keeps everyone awake that is so testing. Then there's his persistent nagging.

'I don't see why we don't stockpile meat for winter.' Again and again Orde-Lees drives the point.

'Because the Boss will be back here before we run out of food,' shouts Wild before storming off. Wild cannot stand any show of pessimism. The mere hint that their sojourn on Elephant Island will be a prolonged one will only serve to erode the men's confidence and sap their ability to endure. Wild knows that his faith in Shackleton is not misplaced, but with each passing week a few of the castaways wonder if Wild's steadfast optimism is looking increasingly like delusion.

CHAPTER THIRTY-ONE

SOUTH GEORGIA, MAY 1916

They hear the puttering of the whale-catcher long before they see it. Mist lies low about the hills but it has cleared from King Haakon Sound. Vincent watches the men row ashore and wonders what they can possibly say to these strangers. Chippy and McCarthy scurry about collecting up their crude belongings. Chippy talks about asking the men to flip the *James Caird* back over and launch it into the water. McCarthy wonders why they would bother.

The waves and shouting carry across the still water. An excited man in an oilskin and heavy fisherman's sweater steps from the rowboat and into the shallows even before the boat hits the beach. He shouts a greeting. There's something about the man that they can't quite place.

Chippy and McCarthy walk forward and shake his hand. Vincent pulls himself from his sleeping bag and shambles on weak legs several metres before stopping, unsure if he is ready for people and conversation.

A few others step ashore and the oilskin man sends them up the beach to help carry whatever paltry belongings will be loaded into the rowboat. The men are Norwegian. They smile and shake hands but don't have any words to exchange despite being surprisingly interested in the lair under the upturned boat where Vincent, Chippy and McCarthy have sheltered for the last four days.

Chippy points to the upturned boat and says in an exaggerated fashion, 'We take it?'

The Norwegians nod vigorously as though there is no question of leaving it. They call to three other men and together they lift the *Caird* back onto its hull and drag the boat down to the waterline.

Despite the prompt rescue, Chippy feels a bit aggrieved. He climbs aboard the rowboat with a sour expression and says to Vincent. 'You'd think our so-called friends might have had the decency to show up.'

Vincent shrugs.

McCarthy looks confused. 'Come on. Can you imagine what they've been through?'

Chippy frowns and says, 'Would have been nice.'

'For goodness sake.' The oilskin man turns in his seat and stares with mock amazement. 'Do you ever stop grousing, Chippy? I could have slept in a real bed last night. Instead I had a bath, shaved my beard off and set back out to sea. I've just spent ten hours on a whaler coming to meet you for breakfast. I can see I needn't have bothered.'

Chippy stares at the man. Minus the shaggy beard and the threadbare clothes, it's Worsley through and through.

Back in Stromness, Shackleton and Crean have undergone a similar transformation. The comfort of clean bodies and borrowed clothes is indescribably wonderful. The comfort of a warm bed with fresh sheets and blankets, though, was too much. Despite their fatigue, neither man could fall asleep. It was infuriating and perplexing and utterly delicious at the same time.

Conversation was tiring. Many locals had got wind of their arrival and had come to shake their hands and hear for themselves the astonishing tale of survival. For their part, Shackleton and Crean had wanted to hear all about the war. When had it ended, who had won. It was with great regret that Sørlle informed them that it was not over. In fact, the situation in Europe had got a lot worse. The fighting was more vicious than ever.

The new day brings fresh challenges. Top of Shackleton's list is a boat to make the trip back to Elephant Island.

There is no question of rest. The steel ship *Southern Sky* is an immediate possibility. Captain Thom is the skipper of another vessel currently in port, but he is available to make the journey. And very keen to help. Finding crew is remarkably straightforward. The whalers of South Georgia are falling over themselves to take part in the exciting rescue. Laid up for the winter, they help fit out the *Southern Sky* and prepare the ship for southern squalls in no time at all.

By 23 May, they are on their way. Despite being buoyed by a sense of adventure, some of the whalers have misgivings. A few of the more experienced hands know that the *Southern Sky* is not a ship for ice.

CHAPTER THIRTY-TWO

MAY 1916

Wild is erecting a flagpole on the hill above the beach. Every fine day they'll hoist the Royal Clyde burgee so the Boss will see immediately upon his return that all is well. It is late May and it won't be long now before they see a ship on the horizon. One of the men holds the little flag up to the wind and it flaps frantically, its golden anchor and lion stark against the royal blue background, a cheering sight overlooking the dismal grey and black sweep of the bay. Wild says he'll present it to the Royal Clyde Yacht Club when they get home.

'Penguins,' says Orde-Lees, who has been assisting Wild with his latest morale-boosting endeavour. 'Scores of them.' His excitement draws the other men's attention away from the task. 'We should really be down there bludgeoning them.'

'Leave them be. We need to finish up here.' Wild's demeanour is as calm as ever, but he's frustrated that the men's focus is now very much on the birds waddling ashore in their little groups. 'Listen, the Almighty hasn't guided us through the greatest ordeals and hazards, only to let us die miserably of hunger here on Elephant Island.'

'God helps those who help themselves,' Orde-Lees says in a priggish tone. He certainly doesn't try to cause annoyance; it happens all by itself.

The spell is broken. The men's interest returns to securing the base of the flagpole with boulders. There's no question, Wild has their loyalty. And, for now, any penguins seeking refuge on shore are safe.

Frank Hurley and Jimmy are also up on the hillside but they're not helping with the construction project. They have another concern. A burial.

'If we're to make any money at all from all this hardship, we're going to need these photographic plates to be in pristine condition,' says Hurley, leaning on his shovel as Jimmy chips away at the hard-packed snow underfoot. After all the care the photographer took of them on the boat, it's just too dangerous to store such treasure in the hut. 'I'll be damned if I let them get smashed, scratched or fouled with all that blubber smoke.'

Jimmy grunts with the effort of breaking the frozen ground. After a few minutes, the physicist's efforts become half-hearted. Hurley seems to have forgotten how impractical Jimmy is. He's the worst man for the job. He lacks focus too. It's not as if he's going to earn a fortune from Hurley's photographs. Catching his breath, he looks down at the windswept bay instead. He feels like he knows every inch of the beach, having walked its length a hundred times or more.

'What's Lees doing now?' he says.

Hurley looks up. 'Those poor penguins. Chased by that deranged lunatic. He never lets up.'

The two friends return to digging their hole. 'It's for the book, the official account of our expedition,' Hurley continues. 'The Boss handed over all the responsibility for exploiting the rights . . . and Frank Wild and I are to do the lecture tour of Europe and America.'

Jimmy shoots Hurley a curious look. 'What about him? What about the Boss?'

Hurley coughs, waves away the comment, 'Yes, well, of course – only if he dies. He'll survive the trip to South Georgia. Of course. All of this will be taken care of by the Boss. I'll be free as a bird to pursue whatever photographic work piques my interest.'

Calculations have been made – the minimum time that it would have taken the six men to reach South Georgia has been discussed ad nauseum, and the earliest that they could anticipate a rescue ship to reach Elephant Island. That date may have passed, but there is no reason to worry. It must be difficult to find a ship both seaworthy and available. Then they will need men to sail the ship, too. That won't be easy with a war on.

Any day, Wild says. Both men take to digging, this time with renewed effort, as if the very act of burying this treasure will hasten that day's arrival.

CHAPTER THIRTY-THREE

JUNE 1916

The ice cave above Cape Wild held such promise, but it is a dismal place to have to spend the day. It is cold as well as wet, but at least it is out of the wind. Conversation passes the hours but makes conditions in the cave worse, with the breath of eighteen men accelerating the thaw. The water drips from the ceiling onto their heads, down the back of their necks, and they wonder how long before they will be called back to the relative comfort of the hut on the beach.

Being soaked to the skin is nothing new for anyone. They recall the early days at Cape Wild when living in an ice cave seemed like an excellent idea, a genuine alternative to the tents, before their hut took shape, before they understood that temperatures would fluctuate wildly depending on the direction of the wind.

The weather is no mystery to them now. They know that a mild west wind is just as likely to bring rain as the cruel southerly is to bring a blizzard to Elephant Island. On the finer days, when the sea mist clears and the scenery reveals itself in all its marvellous beauty, they know that if everything is cleared from the hut and laid out in the open, it might dry out a little: personal gear, the floor cloth, dank and balding reindeer sleeping bags, rancid clothing that in another life would have been incinerated but on Elephant Island is irreplaceable and therefore treated with reverence.

There is no soap to sanitise anything, to lift the grime on utensils or cooking pots or faces. No detergent to tease dried sweat or urine and faecal stains from reeking undergarments. Chances are, no clothing would survive a thorough washing. Such filthy fabric would simply disintegrate. So a good airing is the next best thing. Hands are another matter. They would benefit from a thorough scrub.

'Poor Blackborow, a lad needs his toes.'

'A lad needs his foot, more like it. Better get in there and cut off the rotten bits before the gangrene settles into the flesh. What are a few toes? This ain't no beauty contest.'

'So how will Mack do it?'

'Mack or Mick? Who's doing the honours?'

'Mack's the chopper and Mick's the whopper.'

'No, other way around. Mack's the whopper.'

'The whopper?'

'The one to whop him on the head, to knock him out.'

'You can't be serious!'

There's laughter.

'This will clean out the medicine chest. Anaesthetic, bandages, thread, painkillers.'

'Hope he cleaned his hands.'

'Which one? Mack or Mick?'

'Blackborow.'

More laughter. Jokes to mask the concern. It is a terrible business. Two doctors performing surgery in conditions worse than a field hospital, Wild keeping the feeble flames of the blubber lamps burning, Hurley tending the blubber stove, maintaining the hut at a constant temperature, or as close as he can get it.

If they are called back by suppertime, it will be a quiet meal they share around the stove. Blackborow will need weeks to recuperate, assuming infection doesn't take hold. There are other invalids among them. Not ones requiring surgery; more the services of a psychiatrist. Depression and suicidal thoughts stalk a few of them. Hudson hasn't quite recovered from the sea journey. Rickinson needs constant rest after suffering a mild heart attack.

How extraordinary that, after all they have been through, not a single man has died. It certainly lends hope as they wait to go back to the hut, when they can resume their never-ending wait to go home.

CHAPTER THIRTY-FOUR

FALKLAND ISLANDS, JUNE 1916

Despite the devastating setback, there is no question of giving up. The *Southern Sky* made a valiant effort. But the bravery and determination of the ship's captain and crew were no match for the southern pack ice. One hundred kilometres from Elephant Island, she was turned around. It should come as no surprise – it is winter, after all.

Shackleton has spent a tiresome month in Stanley. The Falkland Islanders are not as welcoming as the whalers of South Georgia. Neither are they interested in accommodating Shackleton's requests for assistance. They complain about the waste. The effort of going to rescue men stuck on Antarctic islands when a war is all that matters. The kindly governor offers to help. If only he had a suitable ship. The best he can do is offer to send a telegram to London.

The British Prime Minister can only do so much. Telegrams crisscross the world, special messengers crisscross the city. A committee is formed and a room is filled with men who have limited interest in the southern ocean and castaways. They decide that it is simply not practical to send a ship. At least until October. Perhaps the Argentineans could be persuaded? If not them, then perhaps the Uruguayans?

The *Instituto De Pesca No 1* is an iron trawler with faulty engines. It comes with a crew of twenty-six and the compliments of the Uruguayan government. They have loaded it with coal and mutton and blankets. On 10 June, it leaves the Falkland Islands with Shackleton, Worsley and Crean, and everyone's hopes of a successful outcome.

Three days later they glimpse the peaks of Elephant Island. A mere 30 kilometres lies between them and their goal. The ice is thicker than it was in May and quite impassable. North-west gales add a dangerous element to their quest. The *Instituto De Pesca No 1* must not linger. Shackleton feels despair. Even more so when he sees the fog that lies so thick about the coastline. While he can see their island, the Elephant Islanders cannot possibly see their leader on the horizon.

CHAPTER THIRTY-FIVE

JUNE 1916

Podgy stomachs, flabby arms, cushioned rumps – it seems odd to have put on weight under such circumstances. But lying around on one's back, eating pure fat three times a day will do that to a man. The 1800 Huntley & Palmer biscuits have been eaten down. What remains will not last much longer. Other supplies are limited.

They may be portly but the lack of carbohydrate in their diets makes the men weak. Catch and kill is their primary focus; penguins mostly, the gentoos that come ashore to digest, bellies almost bursting with krill and fish. The paddy birds and petrels are good eating too, although harder to grab. The paddies are a nuisance: thieving, scavenging. It is sweet retribution to eat them and they taste better than any game bird back home.

The penguin round-up can hardly be called 'hunting'. The penguins squawk in their little groups, surrounded, unable to escape to the sea. A blow to the base of the beak with a heavy club is all it takes. Sixty, seventy carcasses pile up on the beach, ready for skinning. Over a thousand have been slaughtered since the men made this place their home – a ghastly harvest. Nothing is wasted, even the skin and feathers will be thrown on the fire for heat and light, ten or fifteen gone in a day. Green is fed up with all this cooking, being covered in fat, blood, feathers. Day after day he's fried up penguin breasts for twenty-two, stewed up the legs, hearts and livers into a horrible hoosh that the greasy-haired men fall on like dogs, gnawing bones and slurping the watery slop. Somebody needs to take over.

On occasion the men bag a sea elephant. The flesh is similar to the whale meat they ate in South Georgia, only a much darker red. The heart, liver, brains, kidneys and tongues are also edible and considered luxuries when cooked in the same way as offal they might eat at home. There is great excitement whenever one lollops onto their beach. The colossal, slug-like bodies offer a sizeable feed but they are terrifying to take down. The most important thing is the blubber – one thick elephant seal skin can last more than a week.

Sardine tins with a cottonwool wick sputter and smoke, lamps burning with a dull light. It's enough to see the filthy faces of men reading, lying, smoking the latest tobacco substitute, filling the space with an odour of smouldering rope or burning feathers. Talk doesn't often stray beyond their favourite topic: food. Not so much what they're eating as what they would like to eat; what they will gorge themselves on when finally home. Bread and butter, puddings and porridge, a pie crust, apple dumplings, potato mash.

Will their isolation ever be over? Frank Wild certainly believes so. Every fine day starts with his rallying cry:

'Roll up your sleeping bags! The Boss may come today.'

'We'll need enough food to last winter, until August,' Orde-Lees says after their Saturday night meal. 'We should be killing every penguin that comes ashore.'

Wild gives him a withering look. 'There's no shortage of penguins.'

'For now. But later . . . we just don't know. The ringed penguins disappeared the day after we arrived – up and left! And in Bruce's account of the *Scotia*, all the penguins in the South Orkneys were gone by the end of April. There's no telling if the gentoo penguins will also . . .'

'We are not in the South Orkneys.'

'We're on the same latitude.'

Wild holds his hand up. 'Look, even if we did stock up on meat, we've got no way of storing it. It would just rot. We'd all get sick.'

'Not if we bury it in ice from the glacier.' Orde-Lees can't hold his tongue. 'The gentoos can only get ashore while the bay is free of ice. Haven't you noticed? When it's clogged with ice, they stay away. What do you think will happen over winter?'

'Winter!' Wild looks horrified, then trots out his standard line, 'Any day now . . .'

Orde-Lees stops trying to argue the point. He'll never get his way. Besides, to contradict their new leader is not in anyone's interests. He will not convince Wild of anything.

The other men have turned away, started their own murmured conversations. Hussey strikes up a tune on his banjo, keen to start the Saturday night singalong to banish the sense of disillusionment that takes over at the end of another passing week. They'll sing some shanties. Some will recite poems of their own making. The sailors will sing their mournful ballads and Wild will valiantly propose his weekly toast:

'To the Boss and crew of the *James Caird*!'

Nobody has more experience of Antarctic adventuring than Wild, but he's not a born leader. They raise their cups of melted snow spiked with methylated spirits and flavoured with ginger. They are damp and dirty, careworn and cold, living on the most disgusting food imaginable. This is a nightmare and no amount of optimism will banish the worst of fears: it may never end.

CHAPTER THIRTY-SIX

JULY 1916

The days are getting shorter, the weather is worsening and still no sign of rescue. Another factor that is causing considerable concern among the men is the ice building up in the bay. The winter months will all but transform their island into a prison. Any rescue will be problematic. How does one get a decent-sized vessel through pack ice without endangering its crew? It's like their ordeal in the *Endurance* all over again.

And then what happens to our food supply when the wildlife can no longer come ashore? thinks Orde-Lees as he skins and guts the pile of penguins at his feet.

He often volunteers to do the dirty work. In truth, he's grateful for the chance to warm up his hands on the fresh kill. In no time at all, their little bodies will start to freeze, and he will curse the task and the part he has offered to play in it. There are seventy birds to process today, which is a fair number to have to chop up, but they won't last long. One penguin feeds two men for a day. Twenty-two men require eleven penguins a day to sustain them. If they're stuck until August, over 1300 birds will need to be sourced from somewhere.

Orde-Lees has suggested to Wild that they cut rations to half and store what they don't eat. But his words fall on deaf ears. Who in their right mind would want to go without when they are already cutting back on other things? Salt is a luxury, and milk powder is running so low that it must be watered down to a misty liquid that barely carries any flavour. The sledging biscuits are coming to an end. The box they're eating from at present was badly waterlogged on the boats. Under normal circumstances, they'd be considered inedible, but everyone knows a day will come when there'll be none at all.

Orde-Lees shakes his head in dismay. His is the only voice of reason. With practised efficiency he lays the bird on its back and runs his sharp knife from neck to tail. His hands squeeze themselves into the warm, wet abdominal cavity and he gently teases out the stomach and organs.

The liver, kidney, heart and lungs will be put to good use in a hoosh. After setting them aside, Orde-Lees grasps the skin on the front of the bird and tears it from the carcass, taking care to cut around the places where the wings and legs connect to the torso. Placing his boots on the penguin's feet, he leans over and grabs the tail. Pulling with a sharp tugging motion, Orde-Lees zips the skin off the poor beast all the way up to its lifeless head.

The meat is portioned – breast meat, legs, wings, head – and packed into the snow. The carcasses sometimes get boiled up in sea water, but most of them get jettisoned onto a meat pile that they'll only eat if food becomes scarce. The meat pile is a slowly growing mountain of 500 carcasses and Orde-Lees is the only man who eyes it with hope, not revulsion.

The penguin skins are laid out flat for the stove. Orde-Lees takes a moment to wipe his hands and face with the inside of one of the fresh ones. The blubber acts both as a soap and a moisturiser. Squeezing his eyes shut, he braces for the shock of its now-cold greasiness. It slides effortlessly over his dirty face, not so much removing the grime as smearing it over. He gives the raggedy beard that covers his chin and neck a good scrub, then uses the feathered side like a towel, smoothing away the excess fattiness from his features, resigned to the grubbiness of this life.

The hut is the very apogee of disagreeableness. Part of the problem is lack of ventilation. The blubber smoke in the hut has been truly awful. Everyone's faces, hair and clothing are steadily blackening under a glaze of the resinous substance. Their eyes water. They cough. At times their throats feel coated with an acrid layer of pitch. Hudson has developed a terrible hoarse rasp that sounds like bronchitis. Green is suffering the worst case of smoke-blindness of anyone and simply can't cook. The condition is as painful as snow-blindness. He blinks his eyelids rapidly but cannot clear the phantom grit that seems to cover his eyeballs. Deprived of the activity that kept him so busy, he allows himself to slide into a sort of despair. At night, he lies stock-still, not even bothering to move away from the slow leak in the ceiling that wets his sleeping bag. Others position saucepans or tins to catch the drips but not poor Green. He's past caring.

It's not just water from above that makes life uncomfortable. Those who doss down on the lower level have another complaint – the stagnant water that pools under the pebbles that cover the hut's floor. A lot of men initially thought it best to gather up larger stones to lay flat under their sleeping rolls, thinking if they could elevate themselves off the ground they could stay dry, but it doesn't seem to prevent the moisture from wicking into their things. When it rains, it is even worse – they're flooded. They've tried to fashion some drainage channels so the water has a chance to seep away, but the problem lies in the temperature differential. While the ground under the hut is relatively warm, outside the ground remains frozen. Meltwater has virtually nowhere to drain away to. Before long, it backs up to its original level under their sleeping bags.

As cold and uncomfortable as things were while they were floating on the sea ice, at least they could mostly keep dry. Their polar clothing was never meant to repel water, only withstand the rigours of snow in the driest place on Earth. Of course, the layers of cotton and wool offered little protection during the ghastly boat trip; neither do their garments stand up to the damp and squalid conditions of Elephant Island.

CHAPTER THIRTY-SEVEN

PUNTA ARENAS, JULY 1916

Talk in London, back at the Admiralty, has been of leaving the Elephant Islanders for a time; the hope being that their provisions will be more than adequate to sustain them until later in the year. Men who have never set foot on an Antarctic island but have read reports think Elephant Island sounds like a generously stocked hunting ground. Anyone marooned there must have an abundant supply of seal meat.

Telegrams are sent back and forth. Shackleton is mortified at their casual arrogance. He understands the situation. A war is on. Wartime commitments must take precedence.

But he will not forsake his men. And so he will take the rescue on his own shoulders.

Nothing is easy. Nothing is cheap. The *Emma* is a fine and seaworthy vessel. Her twin masts and paraffin engine will see them through. Shackleton hopes the wooden schooner's oak hull will too. The *Emma* costs him eighteen pounds a day to hire. The cook and two seamen are extra. Goodness knows where he'll find the money. An engineer might come in handy. The Boss has heard that the engines are quirky. Two months' provisions will be needed, just in case. The costs mount up along with his anxieties. Thankfully Worsley and Crean are not expecting a great deal other than seeing their companions safe and well again. But that is one thing beyond the Boss's control.

The *Emma* sails on 12 July and makes excellent progress. While the weather holds. Elephant Island is surrounded by impenetrable ice. They will get no closer than 120 kilometres away. The situation is worse than ever.

CHAPTER THIRTY-EIGHT

JULY 1916

Foul weather. The men are confined to sleeping bags and still their teeth chatter. It's a damp cold, far more severe than the thermometer registers. Days are short and the sun never gets high in the sky. Fine days are a rare occurrence. They get one for every ten days of gloom or gales.

Everyone has a gripe. Two or three days of inaction set everyone off, squabbling and snapping. Wordie has an infected hand, Wild has strained his back, Holness and Stephenson have no headroom; lodged as they are on the thwarts in the hut, they can't sit up. Every time they move around up there, a shower of reindeer fur covers the poor blighters in the lower berths. The cook lost two mugs of hoosh through clumsiness and a fight broke out. The man who got it on his sleeping bag is lucky it was not the two petrol cans used for chamber-pots that were upended.

Much trading takes place during inclement weather. It generally involves food. Two lumps of sugar for an extra serving of meat. Nut food is the most precious commodity and it can command a premium. Blackborow promises McLeod seven half portions of penguin steak if he'll swap one bar of nut food. Occasionally patently unfair trades are agreed upon and then disputed, which causes no end of trouble. Wild considers it wiser to outlaw the bartering completely rather than engage in endless negotiations with the wronged party. Besides, he has other crimes to investigate.

Orde-Lees has been heard scoffing sugar in his sleeping bag at night and as he is the man responsible for issuing the provisions, Wild must have a chat with him.

'You cannot be serious!' Orde-Lees squawks.

Wild closes his eyes in exasperation. 'I know. I know. I must admit it's hard to believe. The ones who told me you were helping yourself would be the first to do it themselves if given half a chance.'

'I can account for every single crumb. Even gram of milk powder or sugar. I've shown you the tally-up.'

'Yes, yes, I've seen. If anything, we have more left than I initially thought. Even so, I'm going to have to take responsibility for the issuing of provisions myself. Simply to put an end to this speculation.'

'Speculation?' Orde-Lees spits. 'More like lies!'

Wild holds his hands up to calm the man.

Orde-Lees is exasperated. 'I'll gladly hand over. It's the most tiresome chore anyway. Always having to disappear outside, and in the worst weather. Heading out into a blizzard to fetch things? No thank you!'

Just to add insult to injury, Wild gives the order for the objectionable pile of penguin carcasses to be disassembled and disposed of, as it is both a depressing sight outside the hut and a potential health hazard.

Perhaps a health hazard of a more pressing nature is to be found in the interior of the hut, where an appalling stench rising from the floor threatens to overpower them.

The flat section of the beach where they set up the hut was at one time a penguin rookery. That didn't cause concern. Old feathers and dried penguin guano never hurt anyone. But several months of settled existence have made the men more discerning. And while they've grown accustomed to competing body odours, they cannot stand the reek that arises whenever the thaw water mixes with the putrescent layers deposited by generations of penguins evacuating their bowels.

A foul paste has started to percolate up through the pebbled floor. 'Guano soup', they call it. A reservoir of the evil-smelling liquid pools in front of the stove. Occasionally somebody drops a morsel of food into the mire and must decide whether to pick it out and eat it. More often than not, it is consumed with the regretful words: *waste not, want not*.

On the first fine day, everything is hauled out of the hut. Wordie, Kerr and Orde-Lees lift the floor and remove almost a foot of dirt. Trenches are formed and they collect almost 400 litres of rancid run-off in the petrol cans that at other times serve as chamber-pots. It is a nauseating job to bail out the water but once the unpleasant part is over, they return to a much-improved living environment.

'I would gladly swap places with the average English pig,' observes Kerr as he mucks out.

Wordie raises his eyebrows.

'For his food, his nice dry warm sty with fresh straw.'

Orde-Lees agrees, 'A sty would compare favourably with our shanty.'

Other men search for fresh ground cover. It's not easy with much of the beach now covered in snow. The pebbles are frozen together like raisins in a Christmas pudding. The larger stones nearby have been used for the outside galley; any they find further down the beach are too heavy for men who have grown so unused to physical labour.

Of course, it's a chance to air the sleeping bags, turn them inside out and shake out any debris. Instead of letting it blow to the four winds, the seamen collect up the reindeer fur in case it contains any remnant of tobacco. They shove what they can into their pipes and chuff away on it, convinced that something is better than nothing. It would perhaps be a good opportunity to reassess the sleeping arrangements, but each man has grown so used to the peculiarities of his customary spot that nobody even suggests it. Surely it cannot be too much longer.

CHAPTER THIRTY-NINE

AUGUST 1916

Penguins are a thing of the past. The men eke out their remaining supply and contemplate the rotten spoils awaiting them on the seal carcasses. Bad meat is better than no meat. The end of August is upon them. Every fine day, a troupe climbs Penguin Hill and hoists the flag ahead of the Boss's arrival, but only a very few still believe that he will actually return.

Sending a boat to Deception Island, close to 500 kilometres away, might be the only chance they have of survival. Appointing a crew of men who are physically up to the

269

journey is one thing, but the boats themselves would need considerable work to be made seaworthy. The prevailing winds also pose a problem. How do men take on brutal south-westerly gales with only an old tent cloth for a mainsail? No, such an expedition is a fool's game.

'A month to six weeks,' says Wild with confidence, but it's pure speculation. 'If we leave at the beginning of October, we should reach there at the same time as the first whalers of the season.'

That's a little over a month away. Some might not last that long. Depression, starvation, desperation could easily carry off most of the others before any rescue could be arranged. Blackborow, who has been confined to his sleeping bag for such an extended period, is not at all well. The foot with no toes is horribly inflamed. The pain must be excruciating, but the young man doesn't fuss. Illuminated by the dim rays of the blubber lamp, he looks like a sick child. His eyes follow the conversation, the comings and goings from the hut, but he is largely silent. On clear days, the doctors carry him outside for some sunshine and fresh air, but he cannot cope with the colder temperatures and is soon back in his bag, in his dark corner.

Doctors Macklin and McIlroy are forever grateful that scurvy has not affected anyone, and that their overall slovenly existence has not resulted in a plague of lice or other parasites, dysentery or stomach upsets, but there are other medical issues that require attention. After three days of toothache, Wordie finally gives in to Dr Macklin's urging. A rotten tooth is easier to treat than a festering abscess.

'Make it quick, Doc,' he says before lying back and opening his mouth. Macklin is not the least squeamish. He's amputated toes in the same poor conditions. The back tooth pops out of its angry socket and after the flood of pain subsides, Wordie cradles his jaw. Having little else to occupy him, the geologist will explore the fleshy pocket with the tip of his tongue for the rest of the day. He'd do well to gargle with some boiled salt water, but fuel is strictly controlled now. Along with what little remains of their provisions.

The beach is scoured for supplies. Anything that has been left to languish is retrieved, resurrected, reassessed in terms of its worthiness as a source of nutrition. Marston digs up the partially decomposed bodies of seven paddy birds – a veritable treasure once the grit has been washed off and the birds portioned up.

'Cook them well,' is all the doctors add to the initial debate about whether they're any good.

Recipes are discussed as avidly as ever. Are doughnuts better with jam? Should they be served hot or cold? Should breadcrumbs make their way into puddings? One of the sailors mentions 'sea-pie', Walter How talks of a dish called 'spotted dog', Thomas McLeod concocts a hash of apple sauce, beer and cheese while everyone listens eagerly to how it will taste when he finally takes it from his imaginary oven.

The menu never measures up to their fantasies. The latest delicacy is a soup made from a seal's backbone and flavoured with seaweed and half a bucket of water borrowed from the rockpool. It's an improvisation, necessitated by the fact that the few scraps of meat on their last remaining seal carcass were too putrid to eat. The backbone may have been picked clean but the marrow adds some nourishment, though not much flavour. They slurp and sip, and swap dire predictions about what could be cooked up next.

'We shall have to eat the one who dies first,' somebody offers.

There's laughter.

'Many a true word is said in jest,' mutters Orde-Lees.

CHAPTER FORTY

30 AUGUST 1916

The Chilean navy vessel *Yelcho* slows her engines. The fog has cleared but Captain Pardo will still need to proceed cautiously. He has no idea what rocks or reefs lie hidden on the approach to Elephant Island. This is not his neck of the woods. Worsley has binoculars trained on the distance, Crean just squints with his face set in its usual inscrutable expression. Shackleton has spent a fretful night on the bridge with Captain Pardo, engaged in yet more stressful ice navigation. Deep worry lines lend him an ancient appearance. This is the closest they've ever got. Will they finally achieve what has, up until now, proved impossible? Fourth time lucky.

'Can you see anything yet?' Shackleton asks.

Worsley's concentration is apparent. 'Mmm, no.'

'Fair bit of snow still about,' Crean says, scanning the mountainous island.

'There's the camp!' Worsley says, twiddling the focus wheel.

'Any men?'

Worsley hurriedly hands the binoculars over.

Shackleton clenches his jaw as he peers through the eyepieces. 'I can see two.'

Silence. Crean takes a deep breath.

'Wait, there are . . . six of them,' the Boss says suddenly. 'They're down at the water. I think they've seen us.'

Worsley and Crean look at each other. Could so many have died?

Seen from the shore, the vessel could be anything. The seascape is ever changing. One hundred and thirty-seven days they've been stuck on Elephant Island and the view offers something different every single day.

'Hey Putty, what's that long thing?' Hurley points to the northern horizon.

'I've been watching that berg for months,' says Marston wearily.

'No, beside it. That darker shape . . .'

Marston lifts his eyes. He's struck dumb by what he sees. It's not at all what he expected.

'It's a bloody boat!' Hurley shouts as he bounds off towards the hut.

There's a group down by the waterline, scavenging limpets from the rocks for lunch. They look up at the commotion and wonder if somebody's been hurt.

'Boat!' Hurley hollers as he runs past but their faces just register confusion.

Hurley's rallying cry is met with a good deal more enthusiasm in the hut. Wild throws himself at the door. Others smash out through the very walls into the open, emerging into the daylight like woodlice scurrying from under a dead log. In the mad scramble, boxes are overturned, precious belongings are trampled, and the hoosh pot goes flying. Its contents are sprayed across sleeping bags and books and soak into the ground. Nobody could care less.

Frank Wild runs to the top of the hill carrying the only two tins of paraffin they have left. There's not a moment to lose. He doesn't bother unscrewing the cap, just swings an ice axe over his head like a madman. The liquid glugs out onto the sorry pile of scraps that have accumulated over the last few months. Wild has been living for this day, a chance to set it all ablaze. The beacon burns with a vivid flame. He needn't have worried. The boat is clearly making straight for the shore.

275

Orde-Lees and Hudson carefully carry Blackborow out of the hut so he can see for himself the cause for celebration. Everybody rushes down to the shoreline, waving and whistling and yelling at the top of their lungs. Hurley captures the rapturous scene on his last roll of film. He's frantic with joy at the thought of leaving. He'd better start digging up his cache of glass plates so he can finally share his images of their remarkable ordeal with the world.

The boat is only a few hundred metres from shore, almost close enough to read its name. It is a most beautiful thing to behold and the throbbing of its engines is, by far and away, the most gentle music they have ever heard. Even before the anchor is dropped, two rowing boats are lowered over the side. Wild can clearly make out Crean. And the figure standing on the bow of the other boat is unmistakeable.

As he gets closer, the Boss calls to his second-in-command, 'Are you all well?'

'Yes!' Wild calls back, all the while reminding himself that he should smile, and not just cry.

The men have gathered. Some of them are still holding limpets from the rockpool. Lunch is no longer needed. McLeod takes great delight in flinging his handful into the tide.

'Not one man lost?' Shackleton shouts as he leaps over the side of the rowboat and rushes forward to greet his men. All twenty-two of them. He wants to count them all over again – just to make sure. The explorer has known moments of great excitement and this is one of them. Failing to convey the sheer scale of his relief in words, he throws his arms around Wild. And that is when the tears start to flow.

They need to move quickly. If the *Yelcho* gets stuck, they could face another drawn-out episode in the ice. The turn-around has been swift. Barely two hours and all the men are safely aboard.

Punta Arenas is where Captain Pardo will take them. To Chile, where bells will ring out and flags will be hoisted. There will be people cheering on the quay, and the fire department, the Boy Scouts, the Red Cross, a brass band and every local dignitary will be waiting to greet them. Parties and parades, invitations and speeches – all of it will follow.

'I thought it would take a hundred and twenty days,' he says, grinning at Frank Wild. 'One short Antarctic summer.'

Shackleton's comment is met with Wild's raised eyebrows.

'But it has been six hundred and thirty-five days since we left Grytviken aboard the *Endurance*.'

He looks around at the tangle of dishevelled men on the deck of the *Yelcho*. The smell of them! *Poor blighters, they are a rancid lot.* Some are clutching books or diaries, dark bundles that could be bags or extra clothing. Some engage in excited chatter, some just stare. Shackleton supposes he failed; but it feels like a victory.

'So Frank, this is all we have to show of the Imperial Trans-Antarctic Expedition? Untamed beards and sorry rags.'

'You're bringing back the important bits, Boss,' Wild says.

When Shackleton thinks of all the expedition supplies, food and equipment and animals that took so long to organise and to load, he shudders. Some of it hasn't yet been paid for! Then there is the ship. Lost, but insured at least.

With all the negotiating and frustrations around mounting a rescue, Shackleton has barely had any time for reflection. Antarctica is still an empty circle. And the line he drew through it on the back of the menu? It didn't even get halfway. Shackleton supposes that what he has achieved is just another Antarctic disappointment to add to his list. Nobody even stepped ashore on the continent. If they hadn't got locked in the ice so early and drifted for nine months, if the *Endurance* hadn't got crushed and sunk to the bottom of the Weddell Sea, they might be able to attempt the *last great polar journey* at a later date. Shackleton doubts any of the erstwhile castaways would be interested in joining him on another expedition. Not after spending 166 days adrift on the pack ice, then undergoing a hideous six-day crossing to Elephant Island and then sheltering in a hovel for close to five months. *What a lot a man can endure! In the right company.*

He thinks how fortunate he is to have men like Frank Wild in his life. And dependable companions like Crean and Worsley, without whom he would never have undertaken the 1300-kilometre sea voyage in the *James Caird*, or attempted to cross the uncharted and mountainous interior of South Georgia. Did he ever stop to consider if any of it was possible? Ultimately the Imperial Trans-Antarctic Expedition was a disaster. But perhaps, when all is said and done, he did realise his dream. Against all odds, they did make the last great polar journey.

EPILOGUE

Sir Ernest Shackleton's fight to save his team was not over. On the other side of the continent, ten members of the Ross Sea Party who had been tasked with laying vitally important supply depots in support of the trans-Antarctic crossing were also in dire need of rescue.

Despite their particularly challenging objective, the Ross Sea Party had not received a great deal of guidance from London or financial support to achieve it. Their situation was fraught to begin with, but when their ship, the *Aurora*, broke free of its mooring in Antarctica in May 1915 and was blown 1770 kilometres out to sea, it became precarious.

Stranded with virtually no rations, technical gear or winter clothing, the men were grateful for the shelter offered by Captain Scott's abandoned hut at Cape Evans, where they found a generous supply of food and enough disused equipment to last the winter.

Despite not knowing what had become of their ship and without any guarantees as to their own survival, the ten men agreed that they must carry out their original instructions; to fail to do so would risk the lives of the men on the trans-Antarctic crossing.

All this time, the Ross Sea Party remained unaware that Shackleton's ambitious plan was in tatters. The *Endurance* was frozen fast in the Weddell Sea and drifting northward with the entire expedition team aboard. Nobody would be crossing the continent; nobody would need the supply depots they still felt compelled to lay.

Realising how ill-equipped for travel in freezing spring temperatures they were, the men fashioned windproof garments from old canvas, and footwear from the reindeer sleeping bags they had scavenged from Scott's hut. The second-hand sledges, tents and Primus stoves left from Scott's *Terra Nova* expedition were in a poor state of repair, but would be essential kit for their forthcoming journey across the Great Ice Barrier to the foot of Mt Hope.

On 1 September 1915, they embarked on seven months of arduous sledging that would see them manhaul supplies back and forth over more than 2250 kilometres. By the beginning of autumn 1916, the depots were laid but the men were spent. The return to the coast almost finished them off. Bad weather and ill-health made a difficult journey almost impossible.

The expedition padre, Arnold Spencer-Smith, succumbed to scurvy and was given a hasty burial en route. It seemed a fate they might all share. With their blackened gums and weakened constitutions, others had to be carried on the back of sledges. Once they regained the coast and had access to fresh seal meat they were able to recover some of their strength, but the weather had deteriorated markedly. Scott's *Discovery* hut, where they took temporary refuge, was a rough and frosty abode. Longing to reach the comforts of the Cape Evans hut after months of privations, expedition leader Æneas Mackintosh and dog handler Victor Hayward made a break for home across the sea ice of McMurdo Sound. The two men were never seen again.

Rescue finally came in January 1917. A full four months after he had escorted the Elephant Islanders to safety, Shackleton arrived for the seven survivors of the Ross Sea Party. The depth of their suffering was all too apparent from their haggard faces, unkempt beards and near-hysterical speech. Once aboard the ship, they recounted their incredible tale. Their twenty-month ordeal was every bit as harrowing an experience as that endured by Shackleton and his men on the Weddell Sea. Relieved as he was at having not lost a single man among the complement who sailed with the *Endurance*, the Boss could not claim a similar outcome for the Ross Sea contingent. The three deaths were a heavy burden to carry.

Following their return to Great Britain, many members of Shackleton's *Endurance* crew volunteered for war service and faced fresh hardships on land and at sea. Many had already lost dear friends and relatives to the fighting and were desperate to contribute in any way possible while there was still a war to fight. In the event, two years of conflict remained. There would be ample opportunity to participate before the Allied Forces and the German Empire signed the armistice in November 1918.

Frank Wild was given a temporary commission as a Royal Navy transport officer and sent to Northern Russia. Frank Worsley also ended up in Northern Russia after a stint in the English Channel working as captain of a patrol boat. Tim McCarthy, veteran of the epic crossing to South Georgia aboard the *James Caird*, fell victim to one of the German U-boats that Worsley and his patrol colleagues were responsible for chasing. Seaman Alf Cheetham also died at sea when the ship he was serving on was torpedoed. Thomas Orde-Lees returned to the Royal Marines Light Infantry and later took part in early testing of parachute technology with the RAF. Both Mack and Mick signed up with the medical corps and were exposed to injuries and atrocities that were far worse than anything they'd seen on the ice. Expedition scientist James Wordie was wounded in France, as were four others, although none of them fatally.

Arriving back in England in May 1917, Shackleton threw himself wholeheartedly into the cause of the country still at war. After a period of diplomatic work in South America, he too was sent north, where he helped organise clothing, equipment and transport for troops overwintering in the Russian Arctic at Murmansk and Archangel, where they guarded allied supply depots.

After the war, Shackleton's focus returned south. Once more he would set sail for Antarctica with the goal of mapping over 3000 kilometres of the coastline and scanning the South Atlantic for unknown islands. Once again, finances were tight. His ship was a clapped-out vessel called *Quest*. Its defects and insufficiencies were legion, but Shackleton was ecstatic to be returning to the ice in the company of old friends: Frank Wild, Doctors Macklin and McIlroy, Hussey and superstitious McLeod. But shortly after sighting the first icebergs, Shackleton suffered a massive heart attack and died in his cabin. He was forty-seven years old.

The Boss was given a hero's send-off in Montevideo, Uruguay. He lay in state for two weeks while tributes flowed in from all over the world. It was the express wish of Shackleton's wife Emily that her husband's body be returned not to England but to South Georgia. With only Leonard Hussey of the old guard in attendance, Shackleton was laid to rest in the whalers' graveyard in Grytviken, his head pointing south.

There was never any question in Frank Wild's mind about continuing the journey south. After spending half his life exploring Antarctica, it was finally time for Wild to assume the leadership of his own polar expedition. When once again he came face to face with the ice, Wild rejoiced – as did Mack and Mick and old McLeod, who said quite simply:

'Here we are, home again!'

BIBLIOGRAPHY

Fisher, Margery & James, *Shackleton,* Barrie Books, 1957

Huntford, Roland, *Shackleton,* Hodder & Stoughton, 1985

Hurley, Frank, *Shackleton's Argonauts,* Angus & Robertson, 1948

Mayer, Jim, *Shackleton – A Life in Poetry,* Signal Books, 2014

McElrea, Richard, & Harrowfield, David, *Polar Castaways – The Ross Sea Party (1914–1917) of Ernest Shackleton,* McGill-Queens University Press, 2004

Mills, Leif, *Frank Wild,* Caedmon of Whitby, 1999

Richards, R.W., *The Ross Sea Shore Party 1914–1917,* Scott Polar Research Institute, 1962

Shackleton, Ernest, *The Heart of the Antarctic,* William Heinemann, 1909

Shackleton, Ernest, *South: The Endurance Expedition,* William Heinemann, 1919

Smith, Michael, *Shackleton: By Endurance We Conquer*, One World Publications, 2014

Smith, Michael, *An Unsung Hero: Tom Crean – Antarctic Survivor,* Collins Press, 2009

Thomson, John, *Elephant Island and Beyond – The Life and Diaries of Thomas Orde Lees,* Erskine Press, 2003

Thomson, John, *Shackleton's Captain: A biography of Frank Worsley*, Allen & Unwin, 1999

Worsley, Frank, *Shackleton's Boat Journey*, WW Norton & Company, 1977

Unpublished sources

Blackborow, Perce, lecture notes, SPRI Archive

James, Reginald W, diaries, SPRI Archive

Joyce, Ernest, report of deaths of Ross Sea Party, SPRI Archive

Green, Charles, correspondence, SPRI Archive

Macklin, Dr Alexander, correspondence, SPRI Archive

McNish, Henry, diaries, SPRI Archive

Orde-Lees, Thomas, diaries, SPRI Archive

Shackleton, Ernest, correspondence, SPRI Archive

Wild, Frank, memoirs, Mitchell Library, New South Wales

Wordie, James Mann, diaries, courtesy of Pippa Wordie

ACKNOWLEDGEMENTS

Mounted above the entrance to the Friends Room at the Scott Polar Research Institute (SPRI) in Cambridge, where they serve both morning and afternoon tea, is the only relic of the *Endurance* – the spar that was used as a flagpole on Elephant Island. It stopped me in my tracks twice a day when I was at SPRI researching another polar tale at the beginning of 2019. Not only had it survived the epic journey across ice and ocean, but it seemed astonishing that a man called James Wordie had the foresight to cart this piece of wood all the way back to England. At that stage, I knew a fair bit about Shackleton but almost nothing about Wordie; or for that matter, any of the other men who survived their own epic journey across ice and ocean with the *Boss*.

Thankfully I was in the right place to find out. The SPRI archive is a treasure trove of resources. When it came to writing *Shackleton's Endurance*, I struggled to fit in all the wonderful details I had amassed from the men's diaries, letters and papers that I was able to access thanks to archivist Naomi Boneham, and her assistant Laura Ibbett. Later I would meet James Wordie's granddaughter, Pippa Wordie, who welcomed me into her home in Cheltenham for a few days to look over the fascinating material held by her family.

Two trips to Ireland gave me additional insight and brought me into contact with a vibrant community of polar experts, historians and enthusiasts who gather at the Athy Heritage Centre for the Annual Shackleton Autumn School and finish each day at Frank O'Brien's pub on the square. There can be few places in the world more welcoming to discuss Shackleton, and certainly no finer company!

Top of mind is Michael Smith, author of numerous best-selling books on polar history, including the excellent *Shackleton: By Endurance We Conquer*, and *An Unsung Hero – Tom Crean*. I want to thank Michael not only for reading the manuscript and offering suggestions, but for engaging so readily on a few of the thornier issues I was keen to get right. Another Athy regular, Jonathan Shackleton, also generously contributed his time and knowledge.

I am exceedingly grateful to Sir Antony Beevor for his interest and encouragement from the very early days of the project and for his invaluable feedback in its final stages; but mostly for his friendship. My wonderful mother Helen Cunningham bolstered me with her kind, intelligent and constructive comments when my spirits were flagging, as did my dearest friend Hilary Stichbury, whose sharp wit and red pen can always be relied upon to make things better.

Huge thanks go to my publisher Jodie Webster for seeing fresh ideas and not 'just another Shackleton book', and to my incredible editor Kate Whitfield, whose rigour and sound judgement always fill me with instant confidence. It has been a delight to collaborate once again with UK author, illustrator and dear friend Sarah Lippett, who, despite significant challenges (including a move from London to Edinburgh in this tragedy-filled year of COVID), expressed such excitement in working on another of my Antarctic books.

I am so fortunate to enjoy the good humour and overall robustness of my two sons Kazimierz and Zygmunt. Not only have they had to cope without a mother for extended periods over the last few years, but they have flourished in the process. I love you guys!

And to my husband, Pawel, whose passions are not polar, I must express the deepest gratitude. Over the years his love and support have allowed me to indulge my polar passions without restraint; and without one word of complaint, not even during our month in Antarctica. Thank you Doc! This book is for you.